HIGH SPIRITS

For John,
Here's to San Francisco's historic saloons and the folks who keep them afloat!
JKD

HIGH SPIRITS

THE LEGACY BARS OF SAN FRANCISCO

J. K. Dineen

Foreword by Mike Buhler

Heyday, Berkeley, California

San Francisco Heritage, San Francisco, California

Library of Congress Cataloging-in-Publication Data

Dineen, J. K. (John Kelley), 1968-
 High spirits : the legacy bars of San Francisco / J.K. Dineen ; foreword by Mike Buhler.
   pages cm
 ISBN 978-1-59714-312-7 (pbk. with flaps : alk. paper) -- ISBN 978-1-59714-325-7 (e-pub) -- ISBN 978-1-59714-326-4 (Amazon Kindle)
 1. Bars (Drinking establishments)--California--San Francisco. I. Title.
 TX907.3.C22S3626 2015
 647.95794'61--dc23
                    2015009105

Cover photo and book design: Ashley Ingram
Map design and San Francisco Heritage logo: Chen Design Associates
Photographs: Spencer Brown, Cindy Chew, and Paolo Vescia;
   credits on page 222

High Spirits was published by Heyday and San Francisco Heritage.
Orders, inquiries, and correspondence should be addressed to:

Heyday
P.O. Box 9145, Berkeley, CA 94709
(510) 549-3564, Fax (510) 549-1889
www.heydaybooks.com

Printed in China by Print Plus Limited

10 9 8 7 6 5 4 3 2 1

CONTENTS

FOREWORD

Mike Buhler

"There is only one thing that unites all of the various tribes of San Francisco, and it's not the Giants. It's a love of eating and drinking, and it seems to involve everyone in the city, from San Franciscans who have been here forever to those who just got here Tuesday."

—Carl Nolte, "S.F., a city of restaurants and bars,"
San Francisco Chronicle, April 13, 2013

For generations, San Francisco has been home to a thriving collection of neighborhood businesses that occupy an essential role in the stories and rituals that define the city. These bars, restaurants, cafés, and other places have attracted locals and visitors alike for a taste of the city's unique character and sense of community. They foster lasting social connections as the sites of lifelong memories like first dates, engagements, anniversaries, and retirement parties. From the stiff Bloody Marys served up at The Ramp on the hardscrabble southern waterfront, to the proudly open plate-glass windows at Twin Peaks Tavern in the Castro, to the ceiling mural of famous thinkers at the Philosopher's Club in West Portal, San Francisco possesses a rich food and drink heritage as diverse and colorful as the city itself.

Amid unprecedented economic pressures, these mainstays of San Francisco's cultural landscape are increasingly imperiled by skyrocketing rents and encroaching new development projects. Other establishments are at risk because of perennial challenges that have nothing to do with the current boom cycle, such as retirement and leadership succession.

San Francisco Heritage, or "Heritage," emerged during an earlier era of rapid change in the city, when urban renewal policies resulted in the displacement and destruction of entire neighborhoods. Founded in 1971 with a mission to preserve and enhance San Francisco's unique architectural and cultural identity, Heritage has dedicated itself to advocacy and education over the past four decades, working collaboratively with communities to save the city's historic built environment.

In recent years, threats to San Francisco institutions like the Tonga Room, Eagle Tavern, and Tosca Café have called into question the role of city government—and historic preservation laws—in conserving beloved community anchors that may not be eligible for historic designation. After a hundred years, Chinatown's Sam Wo Restaurant, known for its late-night, no-frills Chinese food, closed in 2012 due to the prohibitive costs of correcting health and building code violations. That same year, the "Save the Gold Dust Lounge" campaign fought mightily to stop the eviction of the storied piano lounge, including advocating unsuccessfully for a landmark nomination. The bar relocated to Fisherman's Wharf in 2013; its former Union Square location is now a chain clothing store. The Eagle and Tosca were spared and have been reinvented by new owners. While cultural touchstones such as Sam

Jordan's Bar and Grill and Twin Peaks Tavern have been declared City Landmarks, historic designation is not always feasible or appropriate, nor does it protect against rent increases, evictions, challenges with leadership succession, and other factors that threaten longtime establishments.

The overwhelming public outcry for saving imperiled legacy businesses highlighted the need for a different approach to conserving the city's intangible cultural-heritage assets. Heritage launched the Legacy Bars and Restaurants project in January 2013 with the announcement of the first round of twenty-five inductees. Our criteria were deliberately loose and flexible, in contrast to the comparatively rigid integrity requirements of historic designation: Eligible businesses must have achieved sustained operation of forty years or more, feature distinctive architecture or interior design, and/or contribute to the cultural heritage of the surrounding neighborhood or the city. Heritage works with business owners to document and promote Legacy establishments through an interactive online guide, a logo and window-decal program, a free printed pocket guide, and special events.

Three subsequent rounds have brought the current total to one hundred certified establishments, with dozens more identified as eligible for inclusion. A public "call for submissions" rallied hundreds of San Franciscans in support of their favorite local spots, with businesses turning to Facebook and Twitter to urge their patrons to vote. "Some people thought it odd," wrote Carl Nolte at the time, when "a very high-class preservationist group organized a vote to select what it called legacy bars and restaurants." But from the very outset, Heritage had hoped that the universal appeal of Legacy businesses would broaden traditional ideas of what is worth saving, to go beyond architectural landmarks to include places that embody intangible cultural values.

Many other global cities have enacted programs and policies to curb the loss of local heritage businesses. In 1998, Buenos Aires, Argentina, launched Bares Notables, an official designation program for bars, cafés, billiard halls, and confectionaries. This served as the inspiration for Heritage's Legacy Bars and Restaurants project. The Bares Notables list grows to include new businesses each year and encompasses both internationally known culinary landmarks and more modest, but no less beloved, local treasures. The city promotes them as tourist destinations, sponsors an annual awards program, and offers grants for preservation projects. In response to the proliferation of tourist shops in certain neighborhoods, the City of Paris has purchased hundreds of properties outright for lease to local businesses for specific uses such as bookstores, artisan shops and workshops, and bakeries. In London, over a hundred pubs have been designated Assets of Community Value. The city's Community Right to Bid program places a six-month moratorium on any proposed sale of designated businesses in order to enable community groups to develop takeover proposals. The Ivy House Pub became the first Community Right to Bid–acquired pub in 2013 and now operates as a cooperative enterprise.

San Francisco's nascent Legacy "movement" can also claim some notable victories: After the Palace Hotel removed the century-old *Pied Piper of Hamelin* painting from its namesake bar in 2013, an online petition garnered 1,200 signatures and testimonials in less than two days, prompting the hotel to quickly reverse its decision. The Maxfield Parrish painting triumphantly returned to its place above the bar, meticulously restored, several months later. In 2015, the city passed legislation to create an official "Legacy Business Registry," the first of its kind in this country. The city registry is directly inspired by, and builds upon, Heritage's Legacy project to include bars, restaurants, retail establishments, manufacturers, arts spaces, performance venues, and service providers that have been in business for thirty years or more. The Legacy Business Registry will ultimately offer a set of financial incentives to registered businesses, as well as owners of properties that house them, to secure their long-term tenancy.

Legacy Bars and Restaurants represents an important milestone in Heritage's efforts to create meaningful new tools, beyond formal historic designation, for recognizing places that embody tangible and intangible cultural values. Bars and restaurants represent only one facet of the city's identity, however, and significant work remains to recognize and sustain the full range of cultural heritage assets.

The stories shared here by the owners, staff and longtime patrons of some of San Francisco's favorite bars, as told by J. K. Dineen, capture the very personal significance of such places, both timeless and ephemeral, to so many San Franciscans.

PREFACE

"Life is a bad item, short but pointless. You stand at the bar playing liars dice with fate. It's the San Francisco way. You might win, and even if you lose, the scenery is great and the weather isn't too bad."

—Herb Caen

The first pubs that I frequented were in the West of Ireland, where my father and some friends from Boston owned a small inn with a bar downstairs. Just a kid, well under the drinking age, I tagged along on trips out to country pubs: I remember the rain-spattered windows, the Tayto Crisps and Pete's Peanuts clipped to racks on the wall, the tangy bricks of peat firing the Stanley Cooker stove. Mostly I recall the talk—the craic and circumlocution, the takedown and one-upmanship. It was the usual topics—gossip, sports, weather, and politics—but there was always a sense that what you said was less important than how you said it. In those days, pubs in Ireland often doubled as suppliers of other provisions—leather goods, groceries, hardware—creating a mix of commerce and camaraderie that brought together rubber-booted farmers and fishermen, town bankers, and long-haired itinerant folk musicians of 1970s County Kerry. At least once an afternoon a hush would descend on the room as someone, often a quiet gray-haired woman in the corner, would deliver a ballad, maybe "The Green Fields of France" or "Carrickfergus."

Those perhaps idealized images of what pub life is all about came to mind in the fall of 2013 when Heyday publisher Malcolm Margolin first talked to me about collaborating with Heyday and San Francisco Architectural Heritage on a book about Legacy Bars and Restaurants in San Francisco. At first I was skeptical—I didn't want to write a guidebook with cocktail recipes and hackneyed lore. Luckily that was exactly what Malcolm and editorial director Gayle Wattawa wanted to avoid. They wanted profiles of places that were shaped by and helped shape neighborhoods: voices on both sides of the plank, the bullshit and the bluster, the sounds and smells, the characters that make sure these particular places endure when so many others have faded from history. They wanted continuity—in some cases it was continuity of ownership, in others it was of clientele or culture that transcended proprietorship.

We started with a list of a hundred establishments that Heritage had recognized as part of its Legacy Bars and Restaurants program. While Heritage had put together a great list, we soon realized we would only have the space to create full-blown profiles of about a quarter of the places on the list. In the end we focused on bars, which, for better or for worse, are more likely than full-service restaurants, bakeries, or cafés to be populated by long-tenured regulars who outlast fads or the fortunes of a particular proprietor. That meant casting aside a lot of my favorite places in San Francisco: steak houses like Alfred's and the House of Prime Rib; roadside places like Beep's Burgers and Whiz Burgers; classic restaurants like Swan Oyster Depot,

The Big Five, Tadich Grill, the Cliff House, Original Joe's, and the Gold Mirror. It meant not covering the Liguria Bakery, Tommaso's Italian Restaurant, Mitchell's Ice Cream, or Hang Ah Tea Room.

The years of establishment you see in this book sometimes speak to when an individual business first got started, like Vesuvio Café in 1948, and other times to when the first bar in a historic space was established, like the unknown bar that in 1858 occupied the space that's now Elixir. In either case, we glean from these founding dates a sense of continuity—a dedication to a space serving the neighborhood as a *bar*.

But even within the world of the city's historic bars, time and space constraints forced us to leave out some noteworthy places including the Bus Stop on Union Street, Pier 23 Café on the Embarcadero, Little Shamrock in the Sunset District, Tommy's Mexican Restaurant in the Richmond District, and Gino and Carlo in North Beach. Regrettably, this meant that some bar owners who were generous with their time still didn't end up with chapters in the book. This includes the artist and waterfront pioneer Flicka McGurrin at Pier 23 Cafe; Frankie at the 21 Club in the Tenderloin; Ron Henggeler, a waiter and historian at the Big Five; Rochelle McCune at Doctor's Lounge out in the Excelsior; and Gabriel Ferroni, third-generation owner of the Bus Stop.

Researching this book also allowed me to get to know some of the city's great bartenders, people whose reputations transcend their places of employment. Many of these folks are quoted throughout the book; others did not make it but still provided me with color. These include Michael McCourt at Original Joe's in North Beach, who attracts what's left of the old Washington Square Bar and Grill crowd from the Herb Caen days. People travel from across the city to see Owen Harrington at the 3300 Club in the Mission. Perry's, the Marina District's pioneering fern bar, spawned several hall-of-fame bartenders, including Paul McCann at the Bus Stop and Michael Fogarty at the Balboa Café.

This book is as much about pictures as it is about the written word, and Spencer Brown and Cindy Chew beautifully captured the spirit of these places. Walking into a bar with a notebook or a camera is not always a comfortable endeavor. The word *pub* may be an abbreviation of public house, but many patrons see their watering holes as private sanctuaries away from the hassles and prying eyes of daily life. At Specs', the bartenders have cards to distribute to overly friendly patrons when warranted. One says: "Sir, the Lady Does Not Wish for Your Attention." The other reads: "Madam, the Gentleman Prefers to Sulk in Silence." As social as drinking establishments are, bars are also places where a person can go to be left alone.

Plenty of friends helped me out with this book along the way. Brian Sheehy, owner of historic themed bars like Local Edition and Bourbon and Branch has been a steadfast supporter and friend since I arrived in San Francisco in 2002. City Hall fixer Dan Dillon knows his way around the waterfront—and its bars. Jocelyn Kane, who runs the city's Entertainment

Commission, put me in touch with owners. Historic preservation consultant Christopher VerPlanck provided insight on several chapters. For the two bars that have received official landmark designation by the city, I relied heavily on the reports that led to that designation. N. Moses Corrette, a preservation planner with the San Francisco Planning Department, wrote the report on Twin Peaks Tavern in the Castro. Stacy Farr, architectural historian with Page and Turnbull, wrote the landmark report for Sam Jordan's with assistance from Tim Kelley Consulting.

There would be no historic bar book without San Francisco Heritage. Executive director Mike Buhler is a trailblazer in a movement to broaden the goals of preservation to include culture as well as buildings. Laura Dominguez, now at Los Angeles Conservancy, shepherded the project with love and finesse, as have Desiree Smith and Renee Cohn. This is the second book I have had the pleasure to write for Heyday. Malcolm and Gayle are literary trailblazers, and I was lucky to have Molly Woodward as copyeditor. I am indebted to my editor at the *San Francisco Chronicle*, Mark Lundgren, as well as executive editor Audrey Cooper, who gave me the time and flexibility needed to pull off a project like this. Finally, this book required tremendous patience and understanding from my kids, Patrick and Mimi, and my partner in crime, Megan Fletcher.

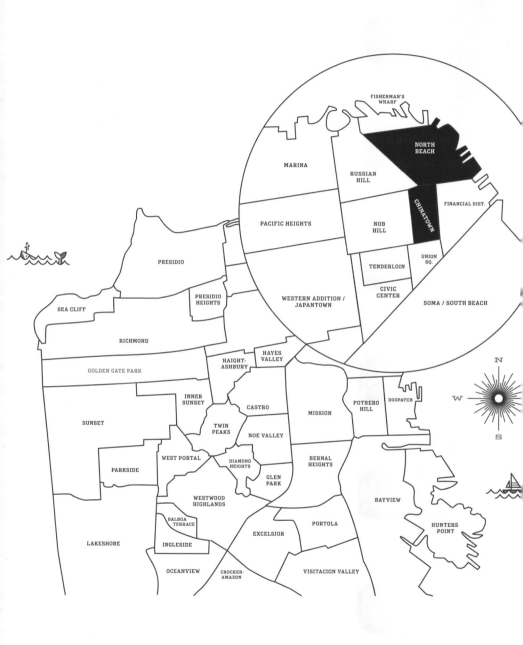

FISHERMAN'S
WHARF

NORTH
BEACH

MARINA

RUSSIAN
HILL

FINANCIAL DIST.

CHINATOWN

PACIFIC HEIGHTS

NOB
HILL

PRESIDIO

PRESIDIO
HEIGHTS

TENDERLOIN

UNION
SQ.

CIVIC
CENTER

SEA CLIFF

WESTERN ADDITION /
JAPANTOWN

SOMA / SOUTH BEACH

RICHMOND

HAYES
VALLEY

HAIGHT-
ASHBURY

GOLDEN GATE PARK

N

INNER
SUNSET

CASTRO

MISSION

POTRERO
HILL

DOGPATCH

W

SUNSET

TWIN
PEAKS

NOE VALLEY

S

WEST PORTAL

DIAMOND
HEIGHTS

BERNAL
HEIGHTS

PARKSIDE

GLEN
PARK

WESTWOOD
HIGHLANDS

BAYVIEW

BALBOA
TERRACE

PORTOLA

HUNTERS
POINT

LAKESHORE

INGLESIDE

EXCELSIOR

OCEANVIEW

CROCKER-
AMAZON

VISITACION VALLEY

NORTH BEACH AND CHINATOWN

VESUVIO CAFÉ, EST. 1948

255 Columbus Avenue

For Vesuvio's sixtieth anniversary in 2008, co-owner Janet Clyde and bartender Tony Lioce organized a literary presentation. The idea was that staff would stand up on the mezzanine balcony and recite verse by the various writers associated with the bar: Jack Kerouac, Gregory Corso, Bob Kaufman, Dylan Thomas, Allen Ginsberg, Lawrence Ferlinghetti.

"I told my wife we were going to do this and her response was, 'Oh great—a bunch of drunks reading poems by a bunch of drunks to a bunch of drunks,'" Lioce said.

It was kind of true: at least half of the poets that put Vesuvio on the map had been booted out of the place.

"We are kind of trafficking in the memory of a bunch of people who were not allowed in here," laughed Lioce, a former rock critic and entertainment editor at the *Los Angeles Times*. "People [at Vesuvio] always want to know 'Is this where Jack Kerouac used to sit?' Well, kinda. But...they kinda threw him out. Or they will say, 'What did Jack Kerouac drink?' You either tell the truth, 'Whatever people would buy for him,' or you say 'What you're drinking right now!' 'Where did he sit?' 'Where you're sitting right now!'"

Vesuvio is a preeminent literary saloon—up there with places like the White Horse Tavern in New York and Les Deux Magots in Paris. That means that distinguished writers both drank there and occasionally even put pen to paper there. Francis Ford Coppola composed much of *The Godfather* screenplay at Vesuvio. Ginsberg has a poem called "In Vesuvio Waiting For Sheila." On October 17, 1955, Neal Cassidy led "the night of howling poets" through the bar, which Kerouac recounted in his novel *The Dharma Bums*. The poets were en route to Six Gallery in the Marina District, where Ginsberg gave the first public reading from *Howl*. It was "the night of the birth of the San Francisco Poetry Renaissance," Kerouac later wrote.

Vesuvio anchors a two-story 1908 Italian Renaissance Revival building in the southeastern corner of North Beach, on the edge of Chinatown. Bright and boisterous, it seems to honk and careen down Columbus Avenue toward the Transamerica Pyramid like a wayward glass double-decker bus. Its facade is a patchwork of stained glass and murals. Twenty-one windows line the curved mezzanine level along the alley to Columbus Avenue. Upstairs, patrons gaze down at City Lights' book-lined shelves or across Columbus Avenue to the flashing neon of porn row: Big Al's, the Condor, the Roaring '20s.

Henri Lenoir opened Vesuvio in 1948. From the start he aimed to create "a bohemian meeting place for artists to come to life." By then he had been around the block—he'd drummed in a big band in the Châteaux-d'Oex, guided tourists in Italy, adjusted insurance claims in Paris, taught ballroom dancing in Nice. Finally, in San Francisco, he figured out what he was good at. "I have no artistic talent myself," Lenoir told poet

Lawrence Ferlinghetti in 1980. "I seem to have a knack, which I can't quite explain, of creating the kind of atmosphere which in a subtle way attracts the creative talent in the population."

After managing a few bars around North Beach, including the Iron Pot and 12 Adler Place, the building at 255 Columbus gave Lenoir a chance to show what he could do. The space he created was "kind and witty" with a "roguish sense of the absurd," wrote *San Francisco Chronicle* architecture critic Allen Temko, who called Vesuvio a "spontaneous San Francisco poem, richer, and far more delightful, than most of the poems that were read there."

If Lenoir had a decorator's flair, he was also a shameless promoter. He sold a "beatnik kit" that included black-rimmed eyeglasses, a beret, sandals, and a turtleneck. In the window he hung a sign that said, *"Don't envy beatniks—be one!"* He hired artist Wally Hedrick to sit in the window and paint as a jazz trio performed. It was good business. "I had a giant beard and attracted tourists," Hedrick said in a 1974 interview for the Archives of American Art.

At first it was a painters' tavern, but soon the poets established a foothold alongside the visual artists. Beats like Gregory Corso and Bob Kaufman mingled with street-corner peddlers of iambic pentameter like Paddy O'Sullivan. Although they helped bring in business, the poets were always controversial, according to Clyde, who said that Kaufman and Corso were "alternatively really interesting and great and then a thorn in everyone's side."

"That is what the poets do—they agitate and push and challenge," said Clyde. "There is tension. You have a couple of ladies who maybe came first [to Vesuvio] in '58 and brought their kids here in '78 and then came back with their grandkids...you can't have a bunch of poets yelling at them that they are capitalist pigs. You just can't have it. You have to make a living."

Today Vesuvio feels neither stuck in the past nor high-minded. Setting the tone is the bar's logo: the rear view of a martini-drinking tattooed imp sitting on a wooden barrel, nude except for a straw hat. It shares a block with a psychic palm and tarot card reading place, the Ali Baba Smoke Shop, and a "licensed Grateful Dead and rock & roll merchandise shop."

Most Vesuvio employees are working artists—something that has been true since the beginning. "Vesuvio is the good ship lollypop. It's got a lot of light. The breezes come through. The art is modern," said Clyde. "People say 'the beatniks are gone, the beatniks are gone.' Well, look around you, the creative people of the day might be serving you."

On the back wall at Vesuvio are Día de los Muertos shadow boxes, little wooden cases with replicas of earthly comforts: fruit, dice, dried roses, coins, cigarettes, and bottles of Fernet. The boxes are meant to soothe the spirits of dead Vesuvio regulars. Morning bartender Josie Ramos, who made the shadow boxes, says she likes the early shift because the ghosts of the previous night are still knocking about. And on a cool, gray summer morning, Vesuvio itself exudes the warmth of

Bartender Tony Lioce

Jack Kerouac

a shadow box. A gas chandelier is suspended above the bar; twenty-one glass Tiffany lamps drip from the ceilings, the stairways, the wooden underside of the mezzanine. At 6:00 a.m. on Sunday mornings, Vesuvio is the most eclectic place in North Beach—exotic dancers from the Broadway clubs mix with taxi cab drivers and early risers who come in with their Sunday *New York Times* crosswords for a Jameson and black coffee.

Vesuvio has a rotating art show, mostly featuring neighborhood painters. One Vesuvio artist is Craig LaRotonda. He walked into the bar with a friend when he first moved to San Francisco in the midninties and got to know Clyde, the co-owner who was a bartender at the time. LaRotonda remembers agonizing over whether to have a show of his acrylic paintings at the bar. "They didn't have any insurance or security and they opened at 6:00 a.m. Anybody could spill beer on the artwork.

I wasn't sure if I wanted to do it. Who goes to bars at 6:00 a.m.?" Eventually, he agreed to hang the artwork. A few days later he received a voice mail from the actor Johnny Depp, who was in San Francisco doing promotion for *Fear and Loathing in Las Vegas*. Depp said he loved the paintings and wanted to get together. The actor not only bought several of LaRotonda's pieces but also introduced him to L.A. gallery owners, which helped him establish a successful West Coast art career. "It was surreal and extraordinary," he said.

Clyde, who headed straight to City Lights Books and Vesuvio when she arrived from Los Angeles in 1978, loves stories like LaRotonda's. It may be a bit of a cliché, but she appreciates that the Vesuvio brand still resonates with aspiring artists, that young poets still show up with a battered copy of *Howl* and a sketchbook and sit at a table on the mezzanine overlooking City Lights Books. She sees herself as the successor to Lenoir along with the Fein family—Ron Fein Sr., who bought the bar from Lenoir in 1970, and classical composer Ron Fein Jr., who today has a majority interest.

"I have to hand it to Ron Fein Sr. for always allowing Vesuvio to be Vesuvio, for never wanting it to follow any trend or change it to be more like another place," said Clyde. "And it was tempting. There were times when business was slow. He held the line, maintained the integrity of the place for everyone to enjoy. That's what we try to do today. To let it be your Vesuvio. Let it be a place where you can relax with your friends, dream your dream."

Poet Jack Hirschman and regular Tony Ry

SPECS' TWELVE ADLER MUSEUM CAFÉ, EST. 1968

12 Saroyan Place

Specs doesn't get to Specs' much anymore. These days the eighty-six-year-old Richard "Specs" Simmons has Parkinson's and stays in an assisted-living tower on Van Ness Avenue.

But the bar still comes to him. Regulars and bartenders bring him pastrami sandwiches and bottles of Bailey's Irish Cream and take him on outings to Marin and Sonoma. "He has all these gorgeous young women constantly coming to see him," said longtime Specs' regular Janine Tong. "I can't imagine what the hospital staff thinks."

Perhaps more than any other bar in the city, Specs' Twelve Adler Museum Café is a reflection of its owner. His spirit imbues the worn wooden floor of 12 Adler Place. It's in the poems scratched out on the round wooden tables; in the décor, the shipping flags, the walrus penis bone, the whale eardrum, the Spanish Civil War posters, the Wobbly memorabilia, the mugshots and drunk-tank key salvaged from the construction site when the old hall of justice was torn down in Portsmouth Square.

"This place is a personification of Specs' personality, his politics, and his inner psyche," said Jessica Soos, a poet who lives above the bar. "It's not just a bar. It's a cultural institution and community space. Specs is one of the most important people in my life, in a lot of people's lives here."

In August of 2014 the Specs' community gathered at the bar for Specs' eighty-sixth birthday. For the occasion friends made up special T-shirts with one of Specs' favorite mottos printed on them: *"For Better Service: Keep moving."* The Specs' gang, drinkers and servers alike, seem to live by that admonition. They are always headed somewhere. Their adventures are spelled out on the thousands of postcards jammed into plastic sandwich baskets on the bar.

> *"It's beautiful at dusk in old San Juan."*
> *"My stories about Malta will be told over drinks."*
> *"Ten days in Pokhara, headed for India."*
> *"I'm surrounded by Italian restaurants and*
> *weirdoes—I feel like I never left North Beach."*

Specs himself was always restless. Born in 1928, he grew up in Boston's Roxbury neighborhood. The men in his family were sheet metal workers or bookies, or both. At fifteen Specs started working afternoons after school making tinware—strainers, cookie sheets, coffee tanks, funnels, milk measurers, brown bread pots for bakeries, drinking cups for the railroad stamped B & M for Boston and Maine. "All those little things that show up in flea markets today," said Specs.

But Specs was never going to be the kind of guy who settles into a family business. From his teenage years he embraced adventure and what he calls "left-wing political crap." In 1948 he signed on with the presidential campaign of Progressive Party candidate Henry Wallace, hitching to California to

organize. After the failed election, Specs bummed back to Boston, hoping to become a merchant marine. The shipping companies wouldn't hire him—he had been blacklisted because of his work for Wallace, who as a candidate had refused to disavow the endorsement of the U.S. Communist Party. Instead he went to Europe for a while, lived in Budapest, played the coffeehouse folk circuit in New York, and eventually headed out to San Francisco. He stayed at what is now the Susie Hotel and got a job cooking at Vesuvio Café, where an old Italian guy taught him to make minestrone soup, frittatas, chopped liver, burgers—"a few good recipes."

"Their lead bartender liked to play the boulevardier, he got drunk too often, so they shoved me behind the bar," he said.

At Vesuvio, Specs met his wife, Sonia. They had two kids, and Specs went back to his sheet metal trade. But after a while he got "sick of swinging a hammer and started looking around for a joint to buy." Finally, in 1968 he took over the lease on the former annex to Tommy's Place at 12 Adler, which in the 1950s had been a pioneering lesbian bar. Specs said he didn't have grand expectations—"just a place for a mixed bag of characters, you know, to see who I could get along with."

At the beginning it was just a bar—there was no inclination that it would become an unaccredited museum of curiosities, natural history, and lefty memorabilia. "In 1968 this place could have been two barrels and a long plank in between. And bare walls. And a beer keg. And gin. And scotch," said Peter Losh, who has been going to Specs' since 1970 when he worked across the street at Discovery Bookstore, now a fortune-teller spot and a head shop.

But customers, especially merchant seamen, started bringing back treasure, and Specs, always handy, built shelving and wooden cases to display the gifts. "Put yourself in his place," said Losh. "You have a successful little bar. You're well loved. Wouldn't people bring you stuff? Wouldn't they send you postcards? That's what happened. Over forty-six years you get a lot of stuff." Specs became close to a merchant marine called Matsumoto, who gifted flags from exotic ports. Specs' friend is immortalized with a sign on the wall: "All dogs on the premises will be turned over to Chef Matsumoto for the Sunday Luau."

Specs' may have gravitated toward merchant marines, but his own nautical excursions didn't go as well. In 1968, not even a year after opening his bar, he joined four other bartenders on a late-night sail from San Francisco to Los Angeles on a thirty-two-foot sloop. They shoved off at 1:30 a.m. Less than an hour into the trip the boat started to sink and the five publicans were left shivering in the choppy sea. They would almost certainly have died had not one of the barmen had the sense to grab a flashlight as the boat was taking on water. The *Examiner* article, tacked to the wall above the trash can at Specs', states: "Five shipwrecked men, visible only because of a single bobbing flashlight, were plucked from the darkened ocean off the Golden Gate early today in a one-in-a-million rescue."

Specs later said that he and his friends were intoxicated enough to be oblivious of the gravity of the situation. "I

Bartender Jacquie

ADLER MUSEUM CAFE

WHAT YOU HAVE TO DO AROUND HERE TO GET A DRINK:

66

remember being in the boat and thinking the skipper's wife was very attractive," he told the *Chronicle*. "The skipper offered us brandy and someone said, 'What kind are you pouring?'"

But if Specs has always been a bit of a wild man, he also has a paternal streak. He is loyal and protective of friends and employees. When he worked bartending shifts he would hand over his tips to whomever he was working with. Specs also encouraged his workers to unionize, which means employees receive health insurance and higher hourly wages. For twenty-five years Specs' most steadfast employee was Kent McCarthy, a six-four, 260-pound, bearded metaphysician. He was Specs' alter ego and surrogate son. He befriended the poets and booksellers from Discovery Books and City Lights across the street. At Discovery, Losh would sell McCarthy discounted philosophy books in exchange for drinks. "'This is a nice relationship we have,' I told him," recalled Losh. "'Yeah,' he said, 'you improve my mind and I destroy yours.'"

On New Year's Eve, 1994, bartender Mark Collins was setting up the bar when a police officer showed up and asked if Kent McCarthy worked there. Yeah, Collins said, he is coming in in a couple of hours. No he's not, the cop said, he overdosed in a residential hotel on Kearny Street. He's dead. McCarthy was fifty-one years old and had spent twenty-five of those years tending bar at Specs'. It was left to Collins to call up Specs at his apartment behind City Lights and break the news. "I was sweeping up the alleyway and Specs came running across Columbus Avenue shouting, 'Tell me I heard you wrong! Tell me I heard you wrong!' I said, 'No, you didn't.'" Specs and Collins went into the bar and spent twenty minutes rearranging chairs. They didn't know what else to do with themselves. Finally, they gave up. "We put a sign in the window: 'Closed tonight. Death in family: Kent,'" recalled Collins. "We put the padlock on the door and went our separate ways."

Kent McCarthy stories are told often at Specs', and his portrait hangs on the wall, not far from the round wooden table where the poets gather on Wednesday nights. Specs' is the de facto community center for what's left of leftist beatnik poetry in San Francisco's North Beach. The poets love Specs because he gives them a simpatico place to congregate. That in turn earns Specs the right to complain about the poets, some of whom, he says, "stopped working when they learned they could get by on bullshit." When the city posted a new "maximum capacity" fire code sign in the bar a few years ago, Specs joked that he was going to put up a second notice: "Maximum Poet Capacity: 1."

That would have cleared the place out.

"Specs has a love/hate relationship with the poets," said Jacquie (Aurora Honeyb Jacqueline) a German-born Specs' bartender. "He likes that they have a home here. This neighborhood is about locals, and they are getting older and things are getting more expensive. At the same time, they move their mouths a lot and don't work too much. Specs has always been a working person, very generous and caring, so it bothers him to see the poets lazing around talking about stuff."

For forty years the poets have been gathering at Specs' on Wednesday nights, a tradition that that grew out of editorial meetings between San Francisco Poet Laureate Jack Hirschman and Csaba Polony, coeditor of *Left Curve* journal. Hirschman, broad shouldered and walrus mustached, buys the pizza for the poets' table. It was something that regular Tony Ryan thought about most when he left San Francisco to live in Washington, DC, for a few years in the 1990s. "Every Wednesday I would think, the gang is at Specs' right now," he said. "I missed it terribly."

That's the thing about Specs', Jacquie said. You can leave San Francisco and travel the world. But you go back to San Francisco and Specs' is still Specs'. "You come back and just pop right back in," she said. "It's like family. Everybody has a place for you. It's a time warp. Nobody gets older in here. Well, they probably do, but in the dim lights you have no concept of time."

THE SALOON, EST. 1861

1232 Grant Avenue

The bent notes of twelve-bar blues drifting down Grant Street—that's how Jon Rochmis discovered the Saloon in the mid-1980s. That's how most people discover the Saloon.

No sooner had Rochmis settled onto a barstool than a pair of bikers in full Hells Angels regalia strode through the bar and planted themselves at the front of the stage. "I was kind of petrified. I was not a worldly kid," he said. "The drummer just stopped playing in the middle of the song. He moved out from behind the kit. He walked over to the Hells Angels. It was tense. I thought, 'Ohhh no, here we go.' Then he gives them big bear hugs. I probably fell in love with the place right then and there."

The Saloon is the oldest bar in San Francisco and it smells like it. It opened in 1861 as Wagner's Beer Hall, under the ownership of Ferdinand Wagner, an Alsatian who landed in post-gold rush San Francisco after a taste of Louisiana. Pictures from the 1870s show a three-story wooden corner structure remarkably similar to what stands there today.

Myron Mu, the reluctant patron saint of North Beach blues, used to play the French horn for a living. He never set out to be a blues impresario. But when his father died he became the Saloon's landlord, inheriting the three-story wooden structure just off Columbus on Grant. Then, in 1984 the bar's owner ran into financial trouble and stopped paying rent. The bar temporarily closed. Worried about the liquor license lapsing, Mu reopened the Saloon himself, thinking he'd just keep it afloat until he found someone more experienced to take over operations. Thirty years later he is still there. "Maybe in the back of my mind I was thinking about a transition from being a performing musician to doing something else," he told *SF Weekly* in 2011.

The L-shaped room has a little stage in the back corner, which regulars call "the back forty." There is room there for about five and a half couples to dance; any more than that and someone is likely to end up in the guitar player's lap. Light filters through stained-glass windows by the doors, which are always open. Outside, a champagne bucket held together with duct tape serves as an ashtray.

The Saloon is known as North Beach's foremost cesspool, a stigma the bar's regulars do everything they can to propagate. Shane, a bartender and doorman, wears Frisco red-and-white biker gear and a large knife sheathed on his hip. In the afternoon, when the blues bands go on at 4:00 p.m., tourists often wander up to the threshold to squint inside. Sometimes they linger there, debating the merits of stopping in for a beer. If they stand and stare in too long, a regular might say, "We're not fucking animals and this is not a fucking zoo." If a tourist comments that the bar "smells," regular Daytime Jimmy might helpfully point out why: "I pissed in that corner and Shane pissed in that corner."

Jimmy is a harmonica player and sometimes construction worker from Buffalo. When he is not collecting a paycheck, he punches the clock at Vesuvio in the morning and the Saloon in the afternoon. He came to San Francisco for a wedding thirty years ago and never made it home. That's the story of a lot of people at the Saloon, he says: "come on vacation, end up on probation." Jimmy is unfailingly polite and doesn't fight because he has an "aversion to pain." Still, he knows that the Saloon is the hardest bar to get eighty-sixed from in North Beach. "You would have to kill somebody—or just about," said Jimmy. "Something a little egregious."

If Jimmy knows the place pretty well it's because he and Shane restored the Honduran mahogany bar a few years back. "The woodwork was so dark you didn't know what was under there," said Jimmy. "The albino cockroaches we shook loose, those made quite an impression, although I've read that every species has a strain of albinos."

Mu owns a few apartments above the Saloon and elsewhere in the neighborhood. He tends to rent to misfits who would not be able to afford North Beach, said Josie Ramos, who tends bar at Vesuvio but used to work at the Saloon. "He picks neighborhood people. He is not a greedy man. If it wasn't for him and his properties throughout North Beach, half of these colorful people you see wouldn't be here."

Blues man Johnny Nitro was one of Mu's tenants—he lived above the Saloon on the second floor. For twenty-seven years Nitro was the Saloon headliner Fridays and Sundays, establishing himself as a regional guitar god who might have found broader commercial success had he been willing to leave North Beach. Nitro combined Memphis R & B with rockabilly. He sang of "drinkin' triples till you're seeing double and feelin' single and gettin' in trouble." In 2011 Johnny died in his pad above the Saloon. His heart gave out on a Saturday night—his night off. The ambulance pulled up outside and word of what had happened spread through the bar. Guitarist Futoshi Morioka stopped playing. "The whole bar went out and lined the street when they brought him down" wrapped in a white sheet, said blues singer Lisa Kindred, who has been playing the Saloon since the 1960s.

Morioka finished the set, playing Bill Withers's "Lean on Me." "Johnny would have wanted that," Morioka told the *San Francisco Chronicle*. "I just played my heart out for him."

The roster of musicians who have stood on the Saloon's plywood stage is formidable: Big Brother and the Holding Company, Quicksilver Messenger Service, Jefferson Airplane, Country Joe and the Fish, B.B. King, Johnny Otis, Boz Scaggs, Aretha Franklin. On any given Friday afternoon you might find Jefferson Airplane founding member Paul Kanter sitting at the bar with a shot of chilled vodka. You might hear Barry Melton, from Country Joe and the Fish. Or Nick "The Greek" Gravenites, who wrote Janis Joplin's Woodstock hit "Work Me, Lord." Or Jinx Jones, who played with Chuck Berry. If Nitro has a successor as King of San Francisco Blues, it would be Ron Hacker and the Hacksaws, "San Francisco's white trash blues icon," who plays on Tom Waits's album *Orphans: Brawlers, Bawlers, and Bastards.*

On a good week the Saloon has live music starting at four and going until one-thirty in the morning. "That's like New Orleans. That's like Nashville, where you can go to a bar in the middle of the day and see a kick-ass band," said Rochmis. "If you want to know what sixties' blues psychedelic rock sounds like—that is what San Francisco music was in the late 1960s—all you have to do is come here and you will hear it."

Rochmis doesn't sugarcoat the Saloon. "It's a dirty, stinky place. They have some of the worst bartenders in the world," he said. "But if you want to hear some music, you come here. So I do."

LA ROCCA'S CORNER,
EST. 1930S

957 Columbus Avenue

"Irish Guys For Chinese Football." That's what the marquee spells out every spring at La Rocca's Corner. The sign is 60 percent baffling and 40 percent mildly offensive. It's all Mike Roddy.

Roddy holds a lot of convictions, few of which would be endorsed by the San Francisco Democratic County Central Committee. One is that the Lincoln High School football team, which his buddy Phil Ferrigno coaches, gets screwed in terms of financial resources. He and some of his friends are abalone divers, so they throw together an annual feed at La Rocca's to sustain the team. They usually raise about $20,000—despite the fact that pretty much everyone at La Rocca's, regulars and bartenders alike, graduated from the city's Catholic high schools: Sacred Heart, St. Ignatius, or Riordan. Or at least got thrown out of those schools.

The public Lincoln High School team is dominated by Chinese American players. "Chinese families are not going to waste money on something stupid like football," Roddy said.

Roddy is a six-foot-five, silver-haired Irishman from the Sunset District. He swims in the bay, coaches rugby, talks trash in his gravelly voice, and delights in rankling the

sensitivities of San Francisco's liberal establishment. He be-friends a lot of young people—construction workers from far-flung places that turn up on the La Rocca doorstep. He got kicked out of the house while still in high school, so maybe he relates to being on his own at a young age. He has seem-ingly been everywhere, crushed grapes in Crete, worked on a Kibbutz in Israel, slept in a monastery in Cincinnati, and inhabited a construction trailer in Revere, Massachusetts.

Roddy used to own Roddy's Fish Bowl out in the Sunset. The bar made sense for him: it was Irish, it was in his neighbor-hood. It resurrected the family name—the Roddys had been bootleggers during Prohibition and owned a half dozen "fish bowls" around the city. But for some reason, Roddy didn't like it. Maybe it was too close to home.

"I made way more money there than I have ever made here. It was packed. We had three bartenders on weekend nights. But I wanted out of there so bad. There were fights every week-end. We had a saying there: 'come for the ahhm*biance,* leave in an ahhm*bulance.'*"

Roddy was spending a lot of time in North Beach and thought he might like to buy a bar there. He swam and worked out at the Dolphin Club, as did his friends the Sancimi-no brothers, who owned Swan Oyster Depot on Polk Street. The Sanciminos were cousins of the La Roccas, a family of musicians who since 1922 had owned La Rocca's Corner, a 1,500-square-foot, three-story flatiron at Taylor and Colum-bus near North Beach's western end. That was Roddy's entre.

"I used to give Leo La Rocca a ride home sometimes." he said. By that time Leo La Rocca was over eighty years old, having been born in 1913 in a little house on Mason Street by Fisherman's Wharf. He had been in the bar business since he was twenty-one, working with his father, Vincente "Papa" La Rocca, and eventually his own sons. The La Roccas were the connected family in San Francisco. It was at La Rocca's Corner that Nick DeJohn, a Chicago racketeer, had his last drink in 1947 before he was found stuffed in his car trunk.

"If you needed a job in the produce market, on a fishing boat, at the garbage depot [then] across the street, they were the people you went to," said Roddy. "It was a cool cat place. Bookies, fight promoters, garbage men, connected characters. That is why you see the sign 'This is it!' Kind of presumptuous, right? It's because people would come here from all over the place. They had heard all about La Rocca's Corner. But when they saw how small and unassuming it was, it would be like, 'This is *it?*'"

In the 1960s La Rocca's was the before-and-after joint for Bimbo's 365 and Italian Villager, which is now Cobb's Comedy Club. Both nightclubs had chorus lines, and the dancers would cut loose at La Rocca's. The La Roccas were entertainers—Leo La Rocca played the banjo; his sons Vince and Jack, the piano and accordion. Socialite Gordon Getty met his wife, Ann, there. Mayor George Moscone hung out there with Willie Brown.

The La Roccas continued to entertain customers into the early 1990s, when Leo La Rocca's generation started to die off.

"The crowd gets older and the music stops," grandson Leo Mario La Rocca told the *Chronicle* when his grandfather passed away in 2006. "That's life."

The bar was "more or less dormant" by 1995 when Roddy teamed up with builder friend Marty Coyne to buy it, said Marte Schreiber, who ran a taco shop next door for thirty years. "It was like a card club, an Italian men's club," she said. Nobody would be in the bar for days—and then suddenly there would be a poker game "and some guy would be getting thrown out the window."

Roddy laments that it is "a donkey bar" now that he owns it. "Before my time it was swinging," he said. "People come in here, sharp-looking people in their seventies and eighties, dressed up, good-looking. They look at me and I can always tell what they are thinking: 'You *ruined* this place!'"

Today at La Rocca's, cable cars rattle by and tour buses idle outside. The sides of the bar's exterior have a lot of hand-painted lettering saying things like "English Spoken," "S.F. Tourist Info," and "Where Tourists and Locals Meet." It's hard to tell if the statements are tongue-in-cheek or serious.

It is true, however, that La Rocca's is full of locals. Every bartender is a city native. Same with the community of bar-owning guys who are part of Roddy's network: Steve Grealish has the Northstar Café and Shanghai Kelly's; Tom and Dick Donahue own the Marina Lounge and the Philosophers Club; the Duggans—John Jr. and Sr.—have Original Joes; the four Sancimino brothers preside over the Swan Oyster Depot.

"All the guys who went to St. Ignatius—they are successes in the bar businesses," said Roddy, who attended Riordan. "If you went to the school I went to...you're not."

La Rocca's even has its native celebrity, the retired boxer "Irish" Pat Lawlor. With his scally cap, goatee, and weathered face, Lawlor is at La Rocca's every afternoon, pacing the bar like it's a boxing ring, picking up glasses, smoking outside on the corner. In the late eighties and early nineties he was a

pretty good boxer—he fought nine champions, including Roberto Durán, Hector Camacho, and Terry Norris. He beat three of them. He couldn't beat his eighth DUI—that landed him in San Quentin in 2008, where he worked on his autobiography, *Fighting My Way through Life*. When there is a lull in the conversation, Roddy might introduce a tourist to Lawlor and fire off a bunch of questions about his fighting career. "Not bad for a kid from the Sunset, right?"

The paradox of the bar business, Roddy says, is that you are happy to see your most enjoyable customers disappear. Between the ages of twenty-four and thirty they might be around all the time; then maybe they smarten up; maybe they cut down on drinking; maybe they fall in love and move away. These days Coyne and Roddy have a good group of kids, including a bunch of nieces and nephews and their friends, just establishing themselves in the city after graduating from college.

"Mike is rough, tough, and socially unacceptable," said Schreiber. "But he has a heart of gold. He is so loyal. He is so proactive about going and doing fundraisers for kids. He takes care of everybody. Trust me."

Sherman Eastsun, a Japanese artist who works out of a garage around the corner from the bar, said he appreciates La Rocca's Corner as "a real redneck bar….These guys are a whole bunch of schoolmates who still hang around together," he said. "Put it this way: they help each other out once in a while. That is what friends are for."

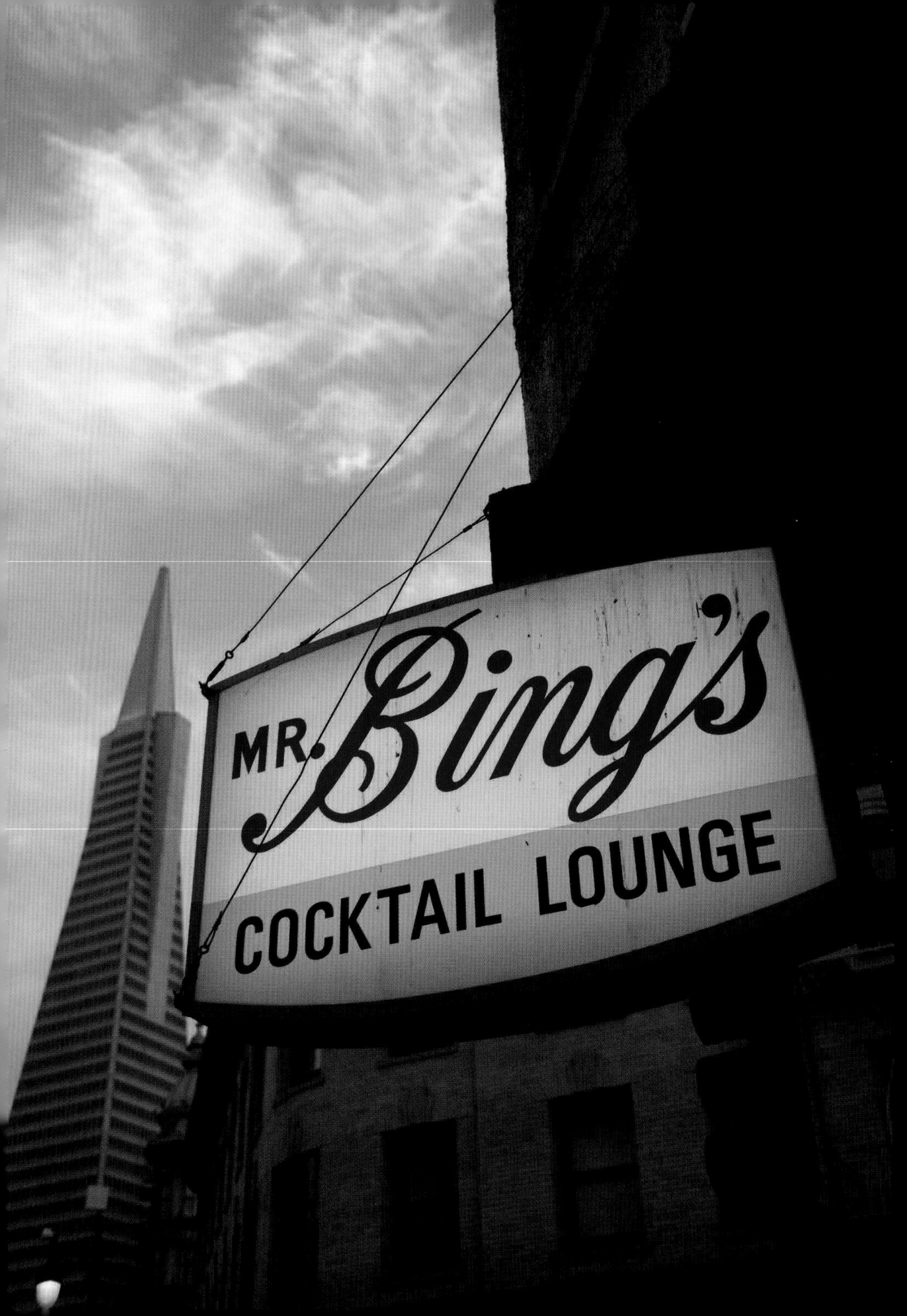
MR. Bing's
COCKTAIL LOUNGE

MR. BING'S COCKTAIL LOUNGE, EST. 1967

201 Columbus Avenue

Mr. Bing's Cocktail Lounge is the most famous dive bar in Chinatown, though after five years behind the bar Conson Hua is still trying to figure out why. It lacks the lacquered red doors, Chinese lanterns, gold Buddha, and cultural pretensions of Grant Street's Li Po, named after a poet from the Tang Dynasty. It is not as old as Red's Place on Jackson Street, which is the oldest bar in Chinatown, or as kitschy as the touristy Buddha Bar.

"What is special about this place? Nothing! It's got one TV, a jukebox, and that's about it! I guess we have fairly cheap drinks, but not even dirt cheap," said Hua. "We have dice, but there is a lot more dice cups around the city than there used to be."

Yet everywhere he goes in the world, people have stories of the Bing, the oddly named V-shaped bar on the edge of Chinatown which, as an *Examiner* columnist wrote in in 2001, affords enough space for two parked sedans with no room remaining for even a "box of miscellany."

After fifty years in business, Mr. Bing looks like he is still moving in. Stacks of beer cases are piled up to the ceiling. There is a cluttered high table in the middle of the wedge-shaped bar area, covered with liquor bottles, glasses, and a cash register with a little American flag sticking out of it. At some point Mr. Bing's featured topless dancers, Hua said. There is a metal ring above the bar from which a cage for the dancers was suspended. Coat check services were offered in the little window in the corner, now boarded up.

Hua says everyone who walks through Mr. Bing's door seems to arrive with a peculiar perspective of what the place is all about, like the woman who showed up recently and looked disappointed after ordering a beer. Hua asked her if everything was okay.

"You're not very rude!" she said.

"I'm sorry?" replied Hua.

"I have read that the bartenders here are very rude, but you're not very rude," she said.

"Oh. Sorry to disappoint you."

Mr. Bing is the nickname of Henry Grant, an eighty-year-old native of Hawai'i who opened the bar in 1965. He still comes by the bar a couple of times a week, usually on his way to the bank. He drives a black Buick with "Mr. Bing" plates. "He is mellow, a little stern, a man of few words," said Hua. "He is very generous with employees, especially at Christmas time."

Mr. Bing originally had an interest in a bar at 155 Columbus, where Comstock Saloon is now. After a dispute with his co-owner, he walked across Pacific Street and signed a lease for the five-hundred-square-foot ground floor space at 201

Columbus. "It took him two years to get his regulars to cross the street," said Hua.

In the early days Mr. Bing catered to merchant marines who stayed at the St. Paul Hotel on Kearny Street. "We were like family—when they couldn't catch the ship, I fed them at my home," Mr. Bing said in 2003 interview.

Mr. Bing's regulars included a man named Kim Chow, who gifted him the one distinctive piece of décor in the bar: a painting on bamboo of a women in a white tennis dress swinging her racquet and scratching her behind. Mr. Bing said the painting, a knockoff of a poster that was popular in the early seventies, was of sentimental value and had brought him good fortune. He said he got frequent offers to buy it—including one for $500. He turned them down. "It was like a good-luck charm, that picture."

The ass-scratching tennis painting was stolen in winter of 2003—a customer ripped it off the wall around last call. The theft was reported in *The Examiner.* Mr. Bing's then daughter-in-law, Rose Fabeo-Grant, hired private detective Don McRitchie to track it down. McRitchie got a tip that the painting was in the possession of a street artist named Rambo, who could be found at a crowded SoMa art opening. When McRitchie found Rambo, sulking in a corner, the artist said he had not taken it but knew where it was. "He told me all kinds of wild stories, none of which I believed," recalled the private eye.

That night about midnight a homeless man brought the tennis lady to Mr. Bing's, wrapped in a green towel. The

Bartender Conson Hua

bartender poured shots all around to celebrate her return. "Now I can rest peacefully at night because I think about that picture quite a lot when I am lying in bed," said Mr. Bing.

Mr. Bing's goes from zero to full in the amount of time it takes to pour a shot of Fireball. The muffled thwack of liar's dice punctuates bar chitchat. On a Friday afternoon in September, the stools filled up with tourists on their way to City Lights Books, financial district bankers on their way home, chefs and bartenders from the Comstock next door. Six Australian rockers came in—skinny black jeans, fat rings, beards, and Mohawks. The night before they had been at Mr. Bing's learning the art of liar's dice, and had decided to come back for more. They were supposed to be on their way to Burning Man. By their well-watered state, it's a wonder if they ever made it to the desert.

The bar became a bit more crowded in 2011 after Anthony Bourdain included it in his Travel Channel show *The Layover,* calling it a "fine drinking establishment." Hua left right before Bourdain staggered in with his entourage. "From what I hear he was his usual self—really liquored up and not that entertaining," said Hua.

Most of Mr. Bing's friends—older seamen like Kim Chow—are either dead or have long since given up drinking. The ones who still come in drink Hennessey VS—Hua just leaves the bottle with them. "They just service themselves and tell me how much they have drank," he said. "There is that level of trust."

DOWNTOWN, TENDERLOIN, UNION SQUARE

LEFTY O'DOUL'S,
EST. 1958

333 Geary Street

The guys at Lefty O'Doul's know how to brighten up the front page on a slow news day. When a veteran Macy's Santa Claus was fired for making an arguably naughty comment, Lefty's was there to save the day, hiring the ostracized Kris Kringle and generating several stories in the *San Francisco Chronicle*. When owner Nick Bovis found Lefty's long-lost, internationally famous Bloody Mary recipe in a golf bag amid cobwebs in the bar's attic, a reporter just happened to be there to witness the discovery. And Lefty O'Doul's may be the only bar in California that hosts retirement ceremonies for police horses, events that never fail to make the evening news. "We roll out the red carpet and get some cute little tourist to give the horse a carrot," said Lefty O'Doul's manager Chuck Davis.

Lefty O'Doul's is as subtle as its slabs of boiled corned beef served up on cafeteria trays. It is unapologetically touristy. It is the last remaining piano bar in a once-rowdy theater district that has become more of a posh shopping destination. Piano bars used to line Geary Street and ring Union Square. There was the Curtain Call, the Theater Lounge, the Geary Cellar, the Gold Dust Lounge, Clancy's Irish Piano Bar, Powell Station, and the High Tide.

"Lefty" O'Doul's RESTAURANT & PIANO BAR

Bartender Chuck D

Davis said there's a reason that these places all died, or at least dumped their pianos. "They were boring as hell," he said. "The same people hit the same places and sang the same one-octave ballads with the same mannerisms. They would run from one piano bar to the next, take the obligatory dollar out and put it in the piano player's tip jar, order their one drink, and stiff the waitress."

The guy who keeps the piano bar routine fresh at Lefty's is Frank O'Connor, a former police officer from Ireland who performs there four times a week. He has regulars from all over the world—one couple from Germany has come for seven straight years, always ending their evenings at Lefty's. Every night it's "Blue-Eyed Girl," "Piano Man," and "American Pie." O'Connor plays the songs differently every night and incorporates the audience. "Friends from Ireland say, 'How long are you gong to stay?' I say, 'Look, they will have to take me out of here in a pine box.' I've never got bored here," O'Connor said.

Lefty O'Doul's is 6,200-square-foot shrine to Lefty O'Doul. From the piano bar up front to the back room with banquet tables and booths, every inch of wall is covered with more than four hundred pieces of baseball memorabilia: Lefty's bats, autographed pictures of Joe DiMaggio (who played for Lefty) and his bride Norma Jeane DiMaggio (Marilyn Monroe), Lefty shaking hands with Japanese Emperor Hirohito, who invited O'Doul to the Imperial Palace.

Lefty O'Doul grew up in the Butchertown district of San Francisco, an area now known as Bayview–Hunters Point. He pitched for the San Francisco Seals of the Pacific Coast League, New York Yankees, and Boston Red Sox, and eventually was converted to a power-hitting outfielder. Upon retirement he returned to the Pacific Coast League as manager of the San Francisco Seals from 1937 to 1951 and served as baseball's goodwill ambassador in Japan before and after World War II. General Douglas MacArthur referred to O'Doul's role in Japan's 1949 postwar recovery as "the greatest piece of diplomacy ever."

O'Doul was flamboyant. He wore a green suit, green socks, green shoes, maybe green underwear. He drove a green Caddy. His first bar was on Powell Street where Kuleto's is now. In 1958 he took over the current location, an empty theater at 333 Geary. He converted it into a Hofbrau, a barrel-shaped bar with cafeteria-style dining. The place demonstrated a flair for publicity from the get-go: on opening day Mayor George Christopher showed up flanked by two Pan American Airlines stewardesses. Actor Eddie Nugent wore a coachman's uniform and played the bugle.

In 1969 O'Doul died. His wife took over operations for a few years, followed by Don Figone. In 2000 Figone announced he was closing Lefty O'Doul's after his landlord doubled the rent to $50,000 a month. "The location has outgrown me," Figone told the *Chronicle*. "Maybe if this was a high-class place with tablecloths, we could afford the rent. But Union Square is turning into Rodeo Drive. All the rents are up, up, up."

Jim Bovis, who owned the Gold Dust Lounge, stepped in and saved it. Today, Lefty's is 60 percent tourists and 40 percent locals—the locals mostly cops, as well as bartenders, waiters, and doormen from the many hotels ringing Union Square. "There are eight to twelve motorcycle cops in here every single morning," said Davis.

On Thanksgiving O'Doul's goes through sixty 30-pound turkeys, and on Saint Patrick's Day serves 1,500 pounds of corned beef. In the spring the Cacophony Society brings the Brides of March, part pub crawl and part parody of weddings in Western culture. The brides test the tequila at the Tunnel Top and tumble down to Lefty's. "Ever been to Goodwill and seen those wedding dresses on the rack? These people go in and buy them. They go to Tiffany's and look at the rings. They go to St. Francis and get thrown out. They go to the cable car turnaround and marry tourists to unsuspecting brides."

One way Bovis makes sure he stays in the news is by featuring reporters on his stage. Once a month Lefty's showcases the Irish Newsboys with *Chronicle* staff writer Kevin Fagan, retired editor Jay "The Hat" Johnson, and KCBS reporter Mike Sugarman. They were playing in July of 2014 when Irish Taoiseach (Prime Minister) Enda Kenny stopped by to see his daughter, who was waiting tables at Lefty's for the summer. Kenny requested "Whiskey in the Jar," Fagan recalled a month later during a show.

"We played this for the Irish prime minister," Fagan said, beginning to strum.

"And he immediately went six thousand miles away," added Johnson.

GANGWAY, EST. 1910

841 Larkin Street

The Gangway on Larkin Street is a bridge to a time when the tough-love Tenderloin was the closest thing gay runaways had to home in San Francisco. Opened a block off of Polk Street in 1910 as a "male-friendly" establishment, the Gangway is likely California's oldest gay bar. The bar sticks out architecturally as well: emerging from the bar's two-tone blue stucco facade is a three-dimensional approximation of a ship's prow, a remnant from a time when the Gangway was packed with service men from the Presidio and Treasure Island.

Inside, the Gangway feels as dim and cozy as a vessel's cabin. And if some of the patrons appear as if they haven't stood on land in a few days, they have the tales to match. Coy Meza, the bar's unofficial historian, says there is a saying at the Gangway: "We judge a smile by its sincerity, not by the number of teeth."

Meza, who curates a bulletin-board history of the Gangway by the bar's front door, said he first stepped into the place when he was about sixteen. That was in the late seventies, one of nine times he ran away from an abusive home in northwest Indiana.

"I kept going until my feet hit water—I couldn't get any farther away from where I came from," said Meza. "Here I found a street family."

Running away was a crime in those days. Every kid hustling on Polk had to cook up a new identity to escape the juvenile court system and make a buck. Meza affected a brogue and became an illegal Irish tough escaping a bad family scene in Galway. He found a place on the bottom rungs of Polk Street's gay nightlife economy: running errands, washing windows, unloading trucks, and moving stock. He knew how to use his fists and was eventually promoted to bouncer and barman at hustler and tranny bars like Rendezvous and Reflections.

Those bars are almost all gone now: The Black Rose, The Polk Gulch Saloon, The Kokpit, Reflections, The P.S., The Q.T., The White Swallow, The Giraffe. The last of them, a hustler bar called Rendezvous, was shut down in 2007 to make way for a congregational church. The only other survivors are Aunt Charlie's Lounge on Turk Street and The Cinch Saloon on Polk.

Today, the Gangway draws older gays with deep memories. On any given afternoon you might be treated to a soliloquy on the origins of The Imperial Council and The Grand Ducal Council, grassroots charitable organizations that raise money through coronation costume balls. You might hear Meza draw on the years he and his husband, Sal, spent as ghostwriters for Bay Area reporter-scribe Dick Walters, also known as Sweet Lips, the Herb Caen of Polk Street.

In his early fifties, Meza is a rare survivor of a generation of Polk Street kids particularly vulnerable to the early days of the AIDS epidemic. In August of 2014 alone, three regulars died.

Regular Tom Trautner

Meza says he has personally been involved in arranging fifty memorial services in the Gangway for friends and patrons who have passed on. A potluck buffet is laid out on the bar. After eating, everyone steps outside and forms a circle. They hold hands and share stories about the deceased. When the recollections run out they take a bouquet of white balloons with LED lights sparkling within and release them into the dark Tenderloin sky.

Meza has vowed to help pass along the history of the old Tenderloin. The Gangway is where that often happens. "We are survivors of a generation that is gone," he said. "There is no glue between the generations on either side of us. You see old queens on their barstools saying, 'What is *she* doing?' And young queens on barstools saying, 'What does that old queen think *she* is doing?'"

At one end of the bar, you can often find Candi Guerrero, who performed from 1963 to 1973 at Finocchio's, the famous female impersonator club. She danced and sang for thousands of tourists, as well as Lucille Ball and Bob Hope, eventually moving to Frolics in New Orleans when Finocchio's traded in real voices for lip-synching. "I did the Arab belly dancing thing, the Brazilian carnival act," she recalled. "I was the Italian sexpot."

At the other end of the bar is Albert Reese, who holds the title Baron to the Blue Diamond Chip in the Imperial Court of San Francisco. "If I am not at home, you can usually find me here," said Reese, a retired property manager. "It's a one-of-a-kind place. Everybody is welcome: straight, gay, tranny. The majority of people here demand something that is not so ridiculous—that people treat them with respect."

When a Korean immigrant named Sukie Lee bought the Gangway in 1998, regulars felt sure that San Francisco's oldest gay bar would become a straight joint catering to younger Asians. Most of the loyal customers, like the seventy-one-year-old Guerrero, were eking it out on a fixed income. They certainly were in no position to buy the craft beers that were generating crowds and profits in the late 1990s.

But as it turned out, they had nothing to worry about. "The gays fell in love with Sukie and Sukie fell in love with the gays," recalled Guerrero. "She was a tiny woman but a ball of fire. When everybody had had a little too much to drink she would make this hot, spicy noodle soup with egg drop in it."

Sukie died of cancer in 2011. She was only fifty. Her memorial, heavy with her beloved disco, set off another chapter of uncertainty. The Gangway is now in a trust held for Lee's college-aged daughter, Winnie. No one knows what will happen to it.

"Everybody is worried that it will no longer be a gay bar, that it will lose its history and its soul," said Meza. "A lot of the people sitting at this bar fought for the right for me and my partner to hold hands. This is a living museum if you are willing to listen to their stories and come in without judgment."

THE PIED PIPER BAR
AND GRILL, est. 1909

2 New Montgomery Street

Just after midnight on March 23, 2013, Joel Sale locked up the Palace Hotel's Pied Piper Bar and Grill, as he had done thousands of times in the twenty years he had worked there. By midmorning the next day, Sale was back at the hotel to open up. He breezed through the polished marble lobby, past the Garden Court with its translucent oblong dome and seventy thousand pieces of glass. With the turn of a key he stepped into the warm wood-paneled barroom.

Immediately he saw something was wrong: above the oak back bar was an expanse of empty wall. His first thought didn't make any sense: Maxfield Parrish's *The Pied Piper of Hamelin* had been stolen. How could that be? The painting was sixteen by six feet. It weighed two hundred and fifty pounds. It wasn't the sort of thing you could slip under your jacket. "It was like I was having a bad dream, like I had somehow walked into the wrong bar at the wrong hotel," he said.

By the afternoon he had learned that during the night representatives from Kyo-Ya Hotels and Resorts, the Hawaiian property owner, had removed the painting and shipped it to New York, where it was expected to fetch between $3 and $5 million at Christie's Auction House. Management was unapologetic. "It is no longer practical for the hotel to display an original work of this value and cultural significance in a public area," the hotel said in a statement.

The backlash was unequivocal. San Francisco Heritage released a statement saying that the removal of *The Pied Piper* "represents a tremendous loss to the cultural fabric of San Francisco." The preservation group took to social media, collecting more than a thousand signatures in favor of bringing the painting back. Mayor Ed Lee called. There was talk of a boycott.

Within a few days the hotel reversed course, announcing that *The Pied Piper* would be returned to the hotel following a museum-quality restoration. While hotel officials were initially ambivalent about returning it to the bar versus another part of the Palace, eventually they agreed that the painting would return to the Pier Piper Bar and Grill.

On August 22, 2013, a crowd gathered as hotel officials ceremoniously rehung the painting. Mike Buhler, executive director of San Francisco Heritage, said a "small part of the city's soul" had been restored. "The Pied Piper Bar and Grill without the painting is simply not the same place," Buhler said. "Now it has been made whole. It really represents the essence of San Francisco."

While not intentional, the threatened sale of the painting turned out to be a hell of a marketing move. San Franciscans showed up who had not stepped foot in the Pied Piper for years. Newcomers to the city popped in to check out the restored piece. Business jumped between 20 and 30 percent.

Bartender Joe Sale

The painting, with its red-capped, flute-playing protagonist luring away twenty-four innocent-looking children, was commissioned by Fred Sharon for $6,000 in 1909. It is one of the most famous pieces produced during the "Golden Age of American Illustration," a populist art movement that included Dean Cornwell and Norman Rockwell. It originally hung in the back "men's dining room," which was not open to women until 1920. It evokes an era when the "New" Palace Hotel, which opened on December 19, 1909—three years after the original hotel was destroyed in the 1906 earthquake

and fire—was a world unto itself, with seventeen barbershop chairs, twenty staff manicurists, and a collection of restaurants that included the Minute Chef, the Tudor Room, and Lotta's Fountain.

The painting is such a focal point, it's easy to miss the bar's other architectural highlights: the hand-laid mosaic floor, the two-story wood paneling, the coffered stained-glass ceilings. The hotel is about to undergo a $30 million renovation, but the bar will be mostly left alone. In fact, hotel management, having learned its lesson, is leaning toward removing the flat-screen TVs from the front bar. "We have gotten to the point where we have a [multimillion-dollar] piece of art in an urban bar and you have TVs next to it," said hotel manager Mark Sneen. "There is an authenticity to the piece that you want to be true to."

Sale, a San Francisco native who remembers peeking through the Pied Piper door at the painting during his senior prom at the Palace, said he would have had to find a new job if the painting had not come home. "To have it back is amazing. When you take away something this valuable and then you bring it back, it has a different meaning."

SOMA AND THE WATERFRONT

THE ENDUP, EST. 1973

401 Sixth Street

The Turtle Brothers used to end up at the EndUp. Now they start their Sunday mornings there.

Three decades after they met on the illuminated plastic dance floor in San Francisco's most notorious all-night club, Mike Geltz and Grant Minix still assume their positions by the bar. They sip their prebreakfast screwdrivers. They hug the servers and bar-backs hustling in and out through the circular bar's little swinging door.

The official name is the Sunday T-Dance. Everyone calls it Church.

"Church made the EndUp what it is. You come here to worship and enjoy," said Geltz. "You come through the door and forget all your problems."

The Turtle Brothers don't look like the after-hours crowd at The EndUp. Their jeans are pressed and their shirts tucked in. Geltz collects turtles. He favors baseball caps with turtle logos. When he and Grant got together thirty years ago, they became the Turtle Brothers.

Like most retirees, the Turtle Brothers reminisce. Unlike most retirees they happen to do the reminiscing in a throbbing nightclub where shirtless men with smooth torsos wave glow sticks. This is what they remember: When it rained they would put out garbage cans to catch the rainwater. Everybody would dance around them. "Two-Shoes" wore mismatched shoes while Philip would hand out tulips on the dance floor after stopping by the San Francisco Flower Mart at Sixth and Brannan. The trannies were always around: the Balloon Girls. Cobalt Blue and Tanya Gold. Grace Jones skinny-dipped in the patio fountain. "Every cop in the city knew The EndUp. Every cab driver in the city knew the EndUp," said Minix. "There is no question about that."

The only question is how the EndUp has managed to survive all these years. The wooden three-story building is so close to the Interstate 80 off-ramp it shakes when trucks go by. It has lived through bankruptcy, two fires, and countless police raids. Developers have wanted to build condos there. Designer drugs brought unwanted police attention and more than a fewambulances. Yet it still stands.

The EndUp opened its doors in November 1973, a time when gay dance clubs were migrating from Polk Street to SoMa. It was wall-to-wall men who packed the place for the Sunday-afternoon wet jockstrap dance contest, later immortalized in Armistead Maupin's 1976 Tales of the City series. In 1979 the EndUp's profile was raised when DJ Wayne approached owner Al Hanken about opening at 6:00 a.m., a ploy to lure in partiers from the nearby Trocadero Transfer. Hanken reluctantly agreed, and Church was in session.

It was a high-energy disco party. DJs like Steve Fabus and Patrick Cowley kept the party going. On Valentine's Day 1984,

The Turtle Brothers

Owners Ynez and Zoltan Steiner

a contest called Go-Go's Wild awarded $100 to the best go-go dancer in a wooden cage. The club kids ruled along with drag queens and performance artists like Trauma Flintsone and Diet Popstitute.

Al Hanken died of AIDS in 1989. The next owner, his brother Helmut Hanken, was killed in a suspicious gun accident in 1993. The next owner, a third brother named Carl Hanken, was a chemist with no experience in the nightclub business. He took over the club to honor his brothers' memory. The club was a mess, half nightclub and half narcotics bazaar. It was bankrupt and owed back taxes. The situation was so dire

that Carl threw the club a funeral in 1994—twenty-four DJs in twenty-four hours. At the last minute the club was forgiven some of its debt and hung on. "It was like taking over Rome after it had burned to the ground," Hanken said. "It was like getting a car that had crashed. The roof was leaking. The sound system was terrible."

In addition to financial distress, Carl faced an ownership challenge from EndUp manager and attorney Douglas Whitmore, who was executor of Helmut Hanken's will. After Carl prevailed in a long court battle, Whitmore showed up at Hanken's house disguised as a delivery guy. Hiding behind two packages, he attempted to gain entry into the house. When Hanken refused, Whitmore shot him four times with a .38. Whitmore eluded police for eleven days, and then shot himself. Carl survived the shooting and is still the EndUp's landlord, though he no longer owns the business.

Today, the Endup is owned by Ynez Stiener. The first time she walked into the EndUp, she was fourteen—a Filipino teenage go-go dancer with a doctored green card and a plausible fake ID. "I came here on Sunday morning T Dance and danced my ass off for years on end," she said. "There was nothing so crazy, exciting, endearing as far as the whole party scene. You felt liberated. You never have to feel alone here. Even if you came alone."

Even as Stiener worked her way through high school and college to become a nurse at a dialysis unit, she never forgot about the EndUp. "Something magical always happened and made me feel whole as a person." She took over the club with a group of investors in 2004. In 2010, she and her husband bought out the other partners. "I couldn't get a loan. The economy tanked. We put hard-earned cold cash into this place. We are in it completely—hook, line, and sinker. If we fail, we fail big," she said.

Stiener was told plenty of times that she would not make it, especially as she aggressively moved to get rid of staff members with their own lucrative and illegal side businesses. She said she had no choice but to clean the place up. She learned every part of the business—how to bartend, DJ, promote. She brought in a trusted nursing friend, DJ Cuervo, to be in charge of promotions and bookings. "I can appreciate that craziness and madness, but we are living in an age where I have to follow rules," Inez said. "We are the only unrestricted after-hours license in the city. Why? Because we follow the rules."

On a good night, a thousand people will roll through the EndUp. DJ Cuervo is in charge of a music program that includes reggae, mash-ups, breakbeat, techno, tech house, and electro house. DJs from around the world appear. While DJ Cuervo knew nothing about electronic music until he left nursing to help Inez out, he has become a star in the industry, spinning at clubs from Dubai to France to Tahiti to Ecuador.

Everywhere he goes, people know San Francisco's EndUp. "Everybody dances together at the EndUp—the million-dollar man and the guy with the Mohawk," he said. "It is like the watering hole in the wilderness. At the end of the night, no matter where the animals have been, they all end up at the EndUp."

DJ Cuervo

THE HOTEL UTAH,
EST. 1908
500 Fourth Street

It was a typical breezy summer Friday afternoon at the Hotel Utah, a 1908 mint-green wooden schooner of a saloon and lodging house run aground at Fourth and Bryant.

Sunlight roasted the bar's northern windows. The Rolling Stones' "Tumbling Dice" played on the jukebox. Outside, musicians unloaded their vans and smoked while the freeway-bound traffic honked on Bryant. The scent of marijuana wafted in through the propped-open door. Down the block to the west, men lined up at St. Vincent de Paul, the biggest homeless shelter in Northern California. A block to the east, construction tower cranes hovered over new condo towers and headquarters for tech firms like Dropbox and Splunk.

Minnesota Bob sat at the bar. So did Shoeless Paul, Toothless Paul, and NASA John, also known as Tequila John. He is both a rocket scientist at Moffett Field and a tequila connoisseur. Carroll Glenn, a fedora-wearing songwriter who generally dresses as if he is going to a funeral, was scribbling lyrics on a napkin while lamenting that he is the only guy at the Hotel Utah who doesn't have a "cool bar nickname." "I guess they call me Cary—but that doesn't really qualify as a cool bar nickname," Glenn said.

The Hotel Utah has the longest-running open-microphone night in California. The roster of performers who have stood on its creaky stage includes Robin Williams and Whoopi Goldberg, PJ Harvey and Nick Lowe, Guns N' Roses and the Counting Crows, Cake and American Music Club. But the Hotel Utah feels more like an Old West way station than a destination or a launching pad. "Three bands a night, seven nights a week, sooner or later the whole world rolls through," said Minnesota Bob.

The Hotel Utah has survived Prohibition, the building of the Bay Bridge, and the slow decline of the smokehouses, breweries, and metal shops that one thrived in the South of Market. It outlasted the bathhouses of the 1970s, the rave scene of the 1990s, the dot-com bust of 2000. The clientele at the hotel upstairs has shifted from itinerant workers to drug addicts to artists to its current mix of tourists and longtime residents.

John Deininger built the Hotel Utah in 1908. He had an exclusive agreement with Fredericksburg beer, which was carted to the Utah by horse and carriage. At the time, the hotel-over-saloon was a proven business model in the neighborhood. A 1914 survey found that forty thousand single men lived in SoMa, only one-third of whom were permanent residents. They lived in residential hotels, ate in cheap cafeterias, and worked in flourmills, sawmills, refineries, machine shops, canneries, printing plants, and breweries. San Francisco's single laborers "enjoyed recreational drinking, worked intermittently, and traveled often," wrote Paul Groth in his 1982 book *Living Downtown.*

By the 1950s the place was run by Al Opatz, a gregarious man who attracted celebrities like Bing Crosby, Joe DiMaggio, and Marilyn Monroe. Al liked beatniks and gamblers but not neckties. If someone wearing a tie got close enough, he cut it off with scissors and tacked it above the back bar. Opatz bought the building in 1966 and renamed it Al's Transbay Tavern, which is mentioned in Francis Ford Coppola's film *The Conversation.* When he met someone he would offer his hand and say, "Shake the hand that shook the world," according to Laura Bellizzi, who has bartended there off and on for twenty-six years.

"He was a funny little guy," she said. "He really would cut your tie off—that's true. He had shot the three elk and one deer up on the wall and felt bad about that. 'Now I just feed them,' he used to say. He was a sweetheart."

In 1977 Opatz sold the building to writer Paul Gaer. By then Gaer had knocked around Hollywood for more than a decade, producing Brian De Palma's *Get To Know Your Rabbit* and writing early versions of the Elvis Presley movie eventually released as the spaghetti western *Charro!* Finally, in 1977 he landed his biggest Hollywood payday with the screenplay for *The Electric Horseman,* which Sydney Pollack made into a movie with Robert Redford and Jane Fonda. Some Hollywood screenwriters use their movie riches to buy a beach house in Malibu. Gaer bought a rundown saloon and residential hotel in San Francisco.

Once he owned the bar, Gaer gave it his undiluted attention. He resurrected the Utah name. He expanded it into an adjacent space that had been a cigar shop and put in windows along the northern facade. In the new space, he built a stage, benching, and a mini-mezzanine accessible from the bar by a little wooden staircase. The new Utah opened on March 18, 1977, with performances by Whoopi Goldberg, Robin Williams, and the Pickle Family Circus. Guy Carson, a touring musician and industry insider, took over booking, and the place became known for "secret shows" by stars playing larger venues like the Warfield Theater and the Fillmore.

Gaer wanted synergy between the bar and the residential hotel upstairs. When he bought the place, the twenty-eight hotel rooms had been overrun by drug dealers and their customers. He worked with police to clean it up, and as rooms

became vacant he would rent them out to artists and musicians. Two of those who rented rooms during that era are still living upstairs—musician Minnesota Bob (Elvin) and photographer Lee Harrison. "Money has never been the bottom line here," Guy Carson told *SF Weekly* in 1999. "We'll leave rooms empty rather than rent to the wrong people."

But it wasn't just music that thrived at the Utah. For twenty years the bar was the heart of San Francisco's photography community. Harrison was one of many employees of New Lab, a photo lab across the street on Bryant. Every afternoon the bar would be full of shooters awaiting their one-hour "rushes." Bar management put in lightboxes behind the bar so the photographers could simultaneously drink and edit.

"It was a community. You knew who was shooting and who wasn't, what they were shooting and with whom," said "Shoeless" Paul Kirchner. "You could run into the Germans shooting editorial, the Milanos shooting fashion, the El Lay folks shooting cars. You knew what assistants to stay away from, what clients were pure hell. When Dan Oshima, the New Lab's client liaison, pulled out the company credit card, you called your wife to tell her you wouldn't be home for a while and don't wait up."

So many photographers occupied stools at the Utah that it became an ad hoc hiring hall for the Academy of Art. "If they needed a teacher to fill in for one of their courses, they would call down to the bar and ask who was around," said Minnesota Bob.

Digital cameras killed New Lab; these days photographers are stuck behind their computers. But it might not have mattered anyway. By the late nineties the dot-com boom was transforming SoMa and driving out the old industries. Fans spilling out of the Giants ballpark brought new nightlife to the area. Whole Foods moved in up the block. Mission Bay started to develop to the south. By 2000 Gaer was ready to retire and sold the bar to Marin-based investors who tried to kill the open-mic night. They wanted staff to wear uniforms. "We called it TGI Utah," said manager Cat Carter, who worked there at the time and returned years later to manage it. "They had no idea what they were getting into—they knew nothing about bars or SROs or San Francisco."

After the dot-com crash, the group sold the Utah to a New York–based investment firm. By December of 2003 every indication was that the bar had reached the end of its line. The new property owners had sued bar management over a rent dispute, and won. The judge gave the bar two weeks to close.

Framed pictures were unscrewed and stacked on the bar along with everything else: Fredericksburg beer labels, Marlene Dietrich movie posters, rusty Utah license plates, a post-1906 earthquake panoramic photograph, a December 1978 Utah music schedule, and back-bar knickknacks like the porcelain palm on which shots of whiskey were placed to toast dead friends of the Hotel Utah. Utah regulars were invited to an Irish wake and were allowed to take home a keepsake.

"I ended up with a little black-and-white picture and a half of a bottle of Dickel's," said Glenn. "There was no outcry, nothing. It was just going away. It was going to be a place that failed."

But behind the scenes, longtime bartender Damian Samuel put together a group of regulars, including two Genentech biologists, to settle what was owed and buy the place. All of the art and artifacts were returned to their places on the wall, and after a short period of darkness the Hotel Utah reopened with the same regulars and the same Monday open mic. Cat Carter returned as general manager in 2008. Her job is as much property maintenance as bar management—replacing rotted wood and averting sewerage disasters. When workers replaced some sagging floorboards behind the bar, they found bullets, old ceramic bottle tops, and bones.

Like in most bars in San Francisco, older regulars like Shoeless Paul and NASA Bob tend to arrive late in the afternoon and clear out before the kids start lining up around nine. There always seems to be a birthday on Fridays, which means cake and champagne. As the sun sets and rush-hour traffic slackens, the regulars start making plans for supper and an impromptu jam session around the corner at Cary's studio apartment.

Bellizzi said that Gaer, who has passed away, would approve. "He ran it like an art project, like he was trying to make something happen," said Bellizzi. "He wanted live music. He wanted a bar full of regulars. He wanted it to be real spontaneous, like a party."

HI DIVE, EST. 1916

Pier 28, The Embarcadero

Owners of old bars learn to step gingerly around the ghosts of saloonkeepers past. One day in 2005, John Caine was at the Hi Dive on fog-impounded Pier 28 ½ when a real estate guy named J.R. Marino came in with a request. His father, Phil Marino, had died. The old man had owned a lot of places around town over the course of fifty years. But of all of the dives and dining rooms he had presided over, the one he had fondest memories of was the Boondocks, which was what the Hi Dive was called before Caine bought it in 2002.

Would it be possible to do a luncheon memorial there in Phil's honor? J.R. Marino asked. Of course, Caine said. He had known and liked Phil Marino, having bought another bar from him at Seventh and Brannan in the early nineties. Caine was touched that on his deathbed Marino had been thinking about the creaky wooden shack in the shadow of the Bay Bridge.

The Saturday afternoon rolled around. The Hi Dive staff hung photographs from the Boondocks era and played Sinatra on the stereo. The waiters and bartenders wore shirts with the Boondocks logo, which Pat McCune, Caine's partner and owner of a sports graphics printing business, had copied from a matchbook. When it came time for friends and family to make remarks, one of the Marino clan pushed away a table from a window overlooking the bay. "They start saying a few words," recalled Caine. "Then I notice an urn. The window is open. The screen is off. And they take the urn and pour Phil Marino right out the window. Nobody had said anything about ashes."

Phil Marino wasn't the first barkeeper to sling drinks at Pier 28, and John Caine won't be the last. Cheap eateries and barrooms have salted the San Francisco waterfront for much of its history, occupying bulkhead buildings and freestanding wooden shacks on the inland ends of piers, according to *Port City,* Michael Corbett's history of the San Francisco waterfront. The places were a necessity because workers had short lunch breaks—twenty minutes in an eight-hour day—and couldn't venture far. Following the general strike of 1934, waterfront establishments proliferated because the previously mandatory 7:00 a.m. "shape-up" was eliminated, giving longshoremen more time to gather for eggs and coffee, or something stronger.

The following year, 1935, the Bayview—what would become the Boondocks and the Hi Dive—opened at Pier 28 ½. Around the same time, Red's Java House went into business at Pier 30 and a place opened at Pier 23. After the container-shipping industry in the 1960s started killing off port jobs in San Francisco, the Boondocks became more of an upscale lunch and dinner spot, drawing executives from Hills Bros. Coffee and Southwest Marine. The bar hosted bus trips to 49ers games at Candlestick Park.

"We had lamb shanks on Friday, ham shanks and lima beans on Tuesday. It was three or four drinks at lunch—Manhattans and old fashioneds—and secretaries calling up, looking for

Owner John Caine

their bosses," said J.R. Marino. "There were crazy attorneys at Pier 28, one of whom took off his clothes one night. He said, 'It's my birthday and I want to drink in my birthday suit.' We pleaded with him for a while and finally I said, 'Look, we'll shake some dice and if you lose you have to put some clothes back on.' We got his clothes back on."

Jim Kennedy bought the place in 1986, and he and his son had it until 2002. It was tough going—a 1993 Embarcadero beautification wiped out street parking, but as of yet there was no Ferry Building or AT&T Park to replenish the customer pool. By the time Caine and McCune took it over, "it smelled like cigarettes and liquor. There was a drop ceiling and carpeting. It was a cave. It was cozy." Caine liked it—he is from Cleveland and on rainy days it reminded him of the Cuyahoga River.

It turned out that Caine's timing was impeccable. The Embarcadero was starting to blossom with the Ferry Building marketplace to the north and the Giants ballpark to the south. Over two thousand Google employees are now across the street next to the Gap headquarters. New condo towers like the Infinity and the Watermark bring customers who think nothing of spending $50 on a bottle of wine.

Today, old-timers from the Boondocks days still come in once in a while to look around. One of them was taken aback when Caine told him a bottle of Bud was $3.75. "What is there today—a horse show?" the gentleman remarked. Caine got a kick out of that. Nostalgia for the Boondocks era is so strong that at Phil Marino's memorial luncheon and ash dispersal, everyone wanted to buy the retro T-shirts McCune had made up for the waitstaff. Caine joked that they had missed a great business opportunity. "You never think to sell at a funeral," he said.

THE MISSION

ELIXIR, EST. 1858

3200 Sixteenth Street

The sign above the door said Jack's Elixir, 1932. Off the bat, H. Joseph Ehrmann knew that date was wrong. When he walked into the three-story wooden building on the northwest corner of Sixteenth and Guerrero, Ehrmann looked at the mahogany bar, the wood paneling, the leaded glass windows. He studied the bones of the building from the Shell gas station across Sixteenth Street. "I said to myself, 'These people have no idea what they are sitting on,'" said Ehrmann.

"There were bumper stickers on the back bar and things stuck onto it with thumbtacks. The place stunk to high hell. The floor was like a trampoline. The back bar had a scant selection of spirits. It looked like it was going under fast," he said. "My goal was to buy a neighborhood bar. Not only was this a neighborhood bar, I saw that it was a real deal Old West saloon, that it was authentic and that it had been overlooked as being authentic."

After Ehrmann bought the bar and investigated its history, he learned that it was even older than he had imagined. A block from the Misión San Francisco de Asis, the northwest corner of Sixteenth and Guerrero has been home to a saloon since 1858, according to the city directory from that year. With the Arroyo de los Dolores Creek running nearby, it was a place to slack your horse's thirst, and your own, after the long

Owner H. Joseph Ehrma

ride over the plank road that cut through marshland from the Barbary Coast. Only the Saloon on Grant Avenue in North Beach is older.

The 1850s was a period of explosive growth in San Francisco. Fueled by the California Gold Rush the city's population swelled from about a thousand to fifty thousand from 1848 to 1858. While most of the development was on the waterfront, an entertainment district grew up around Misión San Francisco de Asis, with saloons, gambling, bullfights, and horseracing. Irish immigrants, who would continue to settle in the area until World War II, started building there. The 1858 and 1859 gravestones of the Ireland-born at the mission graveyard tell the story: James Sullivan, Anthony O'Connell, and John McLean.

While Ehrmann doesn't know who owned the bar during its first fifteen years, he knows that by 1873 the saloonkeeper was Hugh Mooney, who had it until 1893. After Mooney came attorney Patrick J. McGuinness, who owned the property for forty years. Not only did McGuinness have the means to rebuild after the neighborhood burned down during the 1906 earthquake and fire, he was also sophisticated enough to enlist the help of prominent architect Brainerd Jones, who would go on to design the majority of buildings in downtown Petaluma. According to Ehrmann, it was the only bar in post-quake San Francisco to be rebuilt—a bigger, more elegant version—in the same location by the same owner.

McGuinness survived Prohibition (it was a "soft drink parlor" during those years) and handed off the bar to Thomas Sheahan in 1933. Sheahan eliminated the bar's cigar lounge and bootblack stand and converted a stockroom to a women's bathroom, a reflection of the fact that post-Prohibition it became socially acceptable for women to drink in bars.

From then on, the bar had a lot of names. It was the Hunt-In Club, Swede's, La Bandita, and Club Corona, a popular gay/transvestite Latino hangout that shared patrons with the Latino dance club Esta Noche across the street. From 1990 to 1998 it was Jack's Elixir Bar—part of a chain of seven "Jack's" bars around the city—and then a group of Irish investors owned it from 1998 to 2003 but kept the Jack's Elixir name.

There are no algorithms to connect bars with would-be proprietors, but if there were, Ehrmann and Elixir would be a perfect match. Growing up in New Jersey, Ehrmann was drawn to the Old West. He loved Western movies and books, costumes and toys. As he got older he did not outgrow the interest, even writing a paper on San Francisco Victorian architecture while at Boston College.

Ehrmann had worked in construction, which came in handy at Elixir. Beneath five layers of linoleum—the top one was red-and-white checkered—was the original tongue-and-groove fir floor, which had rotted. The redwood-paneled walls were covered in nine payers of paint. "When I sanded it down it was like one of those hard candies that change colors as you suck on them," he said.

Ehrmann's interest in history is evident from the walls of the bar, which are covered with old newspaper clippings, architectural drawings, and maps. He founded the Barbary Coast Conservancy of the American Cocktail. He unearthed historic cocktails like the Boothby—a Manhattan with a champagne float—that was mentioned in the 1930 obituary of Bill Boothby, who authored the 1891 book *American Bar-Tender.*

"It took all kinds of characters to develop these towns, the good and bad. And a good majority drank and needed to socialize to make sense of it all. The excesses of the drunks, the gunfighters, and the hardcore gamblers are the stuff great stories are made of, but the balance of the good with that evil is what makes the stories of the human condition compelling," Ehrmann said. "The beauty of the most well-carved mahogany is balanced by the reality of tent city saloons that kept miners working, trappers trapping, and homesteaders charging west."

Ehrmann wants to operate "an exceptional neighborhood bar." You can get a can of Hamm's and shot of Jameson for $7 or a shot of Pappy Van Winkle twenty-three-year-old bourbon for $23.95. Elixir is open 365 days a year from 3:00 p.m. to 2:00 a.m. on weekdays and opens at noon on weekends. "We don't close early because it's slow. If you fly into SFO on that last flight at 1:05 and say 'Dammit, I need a drink,' I want you to be able to come here. That is the promise of a good neighborhood bar."

CHA CHA CHA AT ORIGINAL MCCARTHY'S, EST. 1933

2327 Mssion Street

In 1992, Texas transplant J.T. Walker was strolling down Mission Street near his apartment when he heard the cadences of old American music emanating from Original McCarthy's. Having grown up around country music, he felt the gravitational pull.

Inside was the longest horseshoe bar he had even seen. It was cluttered with Pall Malls and glass ashtrays, shot glasses and Bud bottles. The bartenders wore white shirts and black ties. Two harmonica players and a guitarist—all well over sixty—held forth near the end of the bar.

At twenty-eight, Walker was the youngest guy in the room by a long shot. He didn't mind. Original McCarthy's was around the corner from his flat, and Walker found himself dropping in frequently, especially weekend nights when the band the Old Timers was in residence, playing standards like "Jambalaya" and "When My Blue Moon Turns to Gold Again."

"I grew up in bars and, for better or worse, I feel comfortable in bars," he said. "I was a transplant. McCarthy's gave me a sense of roots and a connection to people who had been in the Mission forever."

Back in 1992, the gentrification of the Mission District was not the hot topic it is today. Yet even then, Original McCarthy's was already a relic of a neighborhood that had long lost its Irish accent. "We used to say it felt like Limbo in Roman Catholic theology—populated by people who were waiting to pass into another world," Walker said.

The Irish started arriving in California during the Gold Rush, and by 1880 San Francisco had about thirty thousand residents either born in Ireland or born in San Francisco to Irish immigrant parents. The Mission's first Irish parish was established in 1867, St. Peter's at Twenty-Fourth and Alabama Streets. The Mission Promotion Association became a political machine, spitting out leaders like future mayor James "Sunny" Jim Rolph and C. L. McEnerney, head of the Mission Bank.

In 1914, Mission Street was lined with theaters, including the El Capitan, the Tower, the Grand, the New Lyceum, the Rialto, and the biggest, the three-thousand-seat New Mission. There were billiards halls and bowling alleys, five undertakers, and department stores like Sherman Clay and Hale Brothers. Dances were held at the Knights of the Red Branch, the four-story Irish cultural center at 1133 Mission Street.

On December 5, 1933, the day Prohibition ended, Denis McCarthy opened his bar at 2327 Mission Street. A County Cork native, McCarthy built the longest bar in the city, a one-hundred-foot horseshoe bar—fifty feet on either side.

Regulars Pedro Salazar and Michael Nolan

Cook Narlin Meza

The walls were lined with oak booths that could be enclosed with drawstring curtains for privacy. Patrons could push a button and a number would light up, letting the waitstaff know which booth needed service. "You could drink your booze and nobody would see you or judge you," said Jeff Hanford, who manages place today.

After World War II, the neighborhood's Irish residents began trading crowded flats for single-family homes in the Sunset and the Parkside, as well as in suburbs in Marin and San Mateo Counties. The Irish flight freed up cheap housing for Mexican immigrants and for artists. By 1970 the Mission was 45 percent Latino. Calle 24 became the heart of a new Mexican district, as the proportion of Latino businesses along the retail strip grew from 7 percent in 1953 to 32 percent in 1963 to 60 percent in 1973. The Chicano movement flourished, and the neighborhood became known for its bright murals and progressive politics.

Somehow Original McCarthy's hung on—the last stand of the Mission Irish. In addition to the aging Irish population, the bar became popular with the San Francisco Mime Troupe, which operated out of a building around the corner. "It was the local for actors and old Irish people," said Michael Nolan, who was part of the mime troupe and is still a regular at the bar.

By the time he arrived in 1992, Walker, the Texas filmmaker, felt certain that the bar, and its troupe of elderly musicians, would not be around much longer. Walker decided to make a documentary about the bar. The lush black-and-white sixteen-minute film captures a community for whom the bar, and its old-time songs, is a last bulwark against the neighborhood's fading Irishness.

The narrator of the movie, Jack Dowling, put it this way in his Cork brogue: "The majority of the people who frequent McCarthy's are from the neighborhood. Some are elderly now. Retired. Some may drink to excess. They may be old and lonely, not much of a life at home. They just come to McCarthy's because they feel safe there and they are treated all right and understood by the bartenders and the management."

In the film, the older McCarthy's patrons reminisce. One said she knew McCarthy's in the 1930s and would go there before a show at El Capitan. "Beer was ten cents and they would give you a big bowl of beans with it," she said. Another woman said it was the only bar in the Mission she would step foot in. "I will only go where I am known." She added that she used to sing, but had to switch to harmonica. "I'm all sung out," she said.

When the children of James McCarthy (Denis's uncle) decided to sell the bar, they found buyers in Philip Bellber and Leon Pak, the owners of the Cha Cha Cha on Haight Street. Pak, who is of Cuban descent, wanted to do a Cuban restaurant. Bellber, a New Yorker of Puerto Rican extraction who is married to an Irish woman, argued for preserving the Irish legacy. What they ended up with was a hybrid: Cha Cha Cha at

Original McCarthy's. It's an Irish bar with Cuban food, which is better than a Cuban bar with Irish food. The open kitchen in the back of the bar cranks out fried platanos maduros, seafood paella, and Cajun shrimp with pitchers of sangria and enough mojitos that the place goes through a pound of mint on a busy night. Latino bands play on Tuesday nights; regular La Familia Peña-Govea does a Tex-Mex version of Johnny Cash's "Ring of Fire." When Bernal Heights resident Pat O'Shea visits Cha Cha Cha with his sister Katie O'Shea, a nun, they sit at "O'Shea's Corner," the back left table, where Nolan hung a blown-up black-and-white photo from 1957 of their Uncle Barney O'Shea posing with James McCarthy.

The new owners removed the drop ceiling and exposed the original brick walls. They debated tearing out the horseshoe bar, which would have freed up enough space to double the number of tables, according to Hanford. But they decided to keep it. Forty-seven stools encircle the bar and line the open kitchen in back of the bar.

"Nobody makes horseshoe bars anymore because they are not efficient," said Hanford. "But having the bar here creates the place. It's live entertainment. You can watch this guy on his date. You can watch this couple arguing, these people celebrating a birthday. There is nothing else like it."

THE HOMESTEAD,
EST. 1902
2301 Folsom Street

Back in the sixties and seventies, Barry Yops would leave the United States for years at a time, going off to practice architecture in Dublin and London. But the soft-spoken, bearded architect always returned to San Francisco, and when he did, he found himself back in the inner Mission District, where brick warehouses offered cheap office space and the spacious saloon on the northeast corner of Nineteenth and Folsom attracted a steady group of builders and residential designers. "It reminded me of a lot of similar bars from my youth in Detroit. It had a lot of light because of all those windows on the north facade," he said. "It was a simpatico kind of place."

It still is. The name above the door has gone full circle from the Old Homestead to Donington Park to Dylan's and back to the Homestead, but four decades later on Friday afternoons Barry finds himself at the near end of the bar, tossing peanut shells on the tiled floor and drinking Guinness alongside a group of men who call themselves the West Enders. The West Enders talk of building code and British football and cost of lumber and carpeting. The group—including contractor Chris Clyde and architect Richard Pennington—are mostly involved in the building trades and lean left politically.

"We are older, mostly European," said David Siddle, a native of Manchester, England, who lives nearby and works with disabled adults. "Some of us are socialists—I'm a bloody socialist, anyway."

Built in 1902 as the Old Homestead, the bar originally had neighbors that included a leather tannery and a Chinese match factory. The corner was an unpleasant crossroads. In 1918 *Chronicle* columnist E. A. Murphy called it "a particularly unsavory boghole." Poet Sam Booth wrote an ode that included the line: "Upon the corner of Nineteenth and Folsom / there is a pool that smells unwholesome." During Prohibition the place was a speakeasy and brothel, presided over by a woman called Fanny Pearl.

In 1933 Jack Ryan bought the Old Homestead and owned it until 1982. It was the industry bar for PG&E, which has a facility next door. For forty-nine years Ryan cashed paychecks for all the PG&E guys—the utility gave him a stipend for agreeing not to serve the workers before 9:00 a.m. Ryan's

Bartender Brian Smart

forty-nine-year tenure might be among the longest in San Francisco bar history.

In 1982 Ryan sold the bar to Dave Nelson, a British expat who had retired from a career as a long-haul truck driver. Nelson was a major fan of the British car-racing circuit and named the bar after the Donington Park Grand Prix. "He always wanted to own a bar. He put so much work into the place. It was immaculate but it never had the customers like it does now," said Siddle.

Nelson retained the PG&E crowd but had trouble expanding his clientele base. "He had 90 percent PG&E workers on Friday nights," said Siddle. "By Saturday night the bar would shine with polish but there would be nobody here. My wife and I would play darts with Dave and his wife—that was it."

A Welsch writer and actor named Tisch Jones took it over in 1996 and renamed it Dylan's, after the poet Dylan Thomas. It was the city's only Welsch bar. From a mural behind the bar peered Dylan and Caitlin Thomas, Winston Churchhill, singer Shirley Bassey, and actor Anthony Hopkins—all noteworthy figures of Welsch ancestry. During the holidays the bar held readings of Thomas's "A Child's Christmas in Wales." The opening line of Thomas's poem "Do Not Go Gentle into That Good Night" is still written above the bar.

Jones was a committed socialist and held fundraisers for various progressive causes. The bar threw its support behind Green Party candidate Matt Gonzalez in the 2003 San Francisco mayoral race and Medea Benjamin's 2004 campaign for

Father and son Barry and Morton Yops

the U.S. Senate. At the urging of a local Salvadoran immigrant who played on the bar's soccer team, Dylan's raised money to build a school in the Salvadoran village of Las Colinas. "We're just a little neighborhood pub in the Latina district," Jones told the *Chronicle* at the time. "We're just one community helping another community internationally."

In 2006 Jones sold the bar to Los Angeles–based Raub Shapiro and New Orleans–based Rio Hackford, son of Hollywood director Taylor Hackford. The owners, who have stylized dives in New Orleans and Los Angeles, embraced the bar's history. They resurrected the Homestead name and installed molded tin ceilings and dark red velvet wallpaper, serving baskets of peanuts, the shells of which provide a crunch underfoot. They retained the fireplace and the gold lettering on the windows. "There are a lot of new people coming in now that we don't know, but they pay respect to the regulars," said Siddle. "Throughout all the changes, the owners have kept the soul of the community."

Today, the bar retains its idealism. There are fundraisers almost every week at the Homestead—for everything from the San Francisco Fire Department to Toys For Tots to health clinics. "Unlike other bars in the area, there is a real sense of community here, and a lot of people who come here transcend ownership," said bartender Austin Hunt. "That is a unique thing, and as a bartender here I feel a responsibility to keep that in mind and create an environment of inclusion, to expand that family to people who have not been coming here that long."

DOUBLE PLAY BAR
AND GRILL, est. 1909

2401 Sixteenth Street

Pilgrims still come in search of Seal's Stadium fifty-five years after it was knocked down: scholars of sandlot baseball; students of the Pacific Coast League; fans of the old pre-San Francisco New York Giants, of Willie Mays and Lefty O'Doul, of the DiMaggio brothers Dom, Vince, and Joe.

They poke around what is now the Potrero Center, a strip mall perched at a crossroads between the Mission District, Potrero Hill, and South of Market. On the corner of Sixteenth and Bryant a plaque tells them that West Coast Major League Baseball started here in 1958. From there, they use their imagination. In 2010 two writers, Todd Lapin and Burrito Justice, employed Google Earth and its historical map overlay to calculate the precise location of Seal's Stadium's bases in the current cityscape. They determined that home plate and first base are in Office Depot, second base is in Starbucks, and to round third base one would run down Safeway's aisle 3, by the frozen pizzas.

Anyone who cares about the history of West Coast baseball eventually ends up at the Double Play Bar and Grill. Fifty feet from what was the right-field bleachers at Seal's Stadium, the Double Play may be the only sports bar in the United States that derives its identity from a stadium that disappeared during the Eisenhower administration. James Moore, a New Yorker who remained a Giants fan even after they abandoned the Polo Grounds in Upper Manhattan for San Francisco in 1958, said he makes semiannual trips to the Double Play. "In what other city would they tear down the stadium, and fifty years later the fans are still across the street, boozing?" said Moore. "You gotta love San Francisco."

Seals Stadium opened in 1931. It was, obviously, home of the San Francisco Seals, who left for Phoenix in 1957, and the Mission Reds, who decamped for Hollywood in 1937. The San Francisco Giants occupied it during their first two years in the city, while Candlestick Park was under construction. Across the street, James Larkin built a three-story wood-and-brick building in 1909, operating the bar and living upstairs with his extended family. In 1937 he sold it to the Stanfel family, owners of a nearby bakery. The Stanfels embraced baseball, changing the name to the Double Play to court ballplayers—Joe DiMaggio, Dario Lodigiani, Bobby Layne, and Doak Walker all went there after ballgames. The bar was so close to the ballpark that right fielders would occasionally sneak across the street between innings for a bracer.

The Double Play still serves baseball nostalgia on tap, but it is as much about the city's neighborhoods and its people as the national pastime. Antique baseball gloves are nailed to the wall, along with photos of Seals Stadium, a scorebook from the 1947 Seals, and a picture of Mel Ott and Lefty O'Doul shaking

Chef and owner Rafael Hernandez

hands. Just as prominent is the local stuff—high school team pictures from Mission High, Sacred Heart, St. Ignatius. Framed portraits of local boxers like Irish Pat Lawlor hang next to police badges from every imaginable branch of law enforcement in Northern California.

Over the last thirty years the Double Play has been shaped by three of San Francisco's great ethnic traditions: Italian, Irish, and Mexican. From the mid-1980s to 2006 Gigi Fiorucci operated it with his son Gino, expanding the bar food menu with a full selection of pastas and Italian specialties. Fiorucci, who owned Mayes Oyster House on Polk Street, added a 1,200-square-foot room in the back, which was used for special events and private parties. He commissioned an artist to do a mural there—a Seals Stadium scene with a team made up entirely of lefties.

Fiorucci's best move may have been to hire Rafael Hernandez to run the kitchen. Hernandez arrived in San Francisco from Mexico in the early 1980s and rose from dishwasher at the Old Clam House to cook at Mayes. For years Hernandez worked two shifts a day—lunch at the Double Play and dinner at Mayes. In 2006 Fiorucci sold the bar to Marty and Tommy Coyne, construction and bar guys who are scions of a large and well-known San Francisco Irish family. Three years later they passed it on to Hernandez and his son Rafael Hernandez Jr.

"Rafa" still lives in an apartment on Valencia, next to the playground. He has raised four kids there. He doesn't drive;

he gets around on a BMW—Bus, Muni, Walk. In the kitchen he makes everything from scratch. His wife, Christina, waits tables and Rafael Jr. works the bar every day from 7:00 a.m. to 3:00 p.m. Working seven days a week he has sent his kids to some of the most prestigious schools in the city, Children's Day School and Sacred Heart.

"I have been coming here since before I would walk," said the younger Hernandez. "My first job was pouring ice teas, waters, and bringing bread to the tables."

Today, the Double Play is still a sports bar—the ceiling is stained with champagne spray from the Giants' three recent championships. Rafael Jr., a 2006 graduate of Sacred Heart, draws a new generation of San Francisco natives, many of whom have moved back to the city after college. The bar crowd shifts with the ever-changing neighborhood employment base. The Parisian Bakery and Wonder Bread factory at 1525 Bryant closed in 2005, becoming a U-Haul self-storage facility. Bode Concrete moved and was replace by condos. The old Hamm's Brewery is a Sports Basement.

Night nurses come into the Double Play from San Francisco General Hospital, and the bar is close enough to the police headquarters and jail at 850 Bryant that it attracts cops from all over the city. Letter carriers from the post office on Bryant Street remain an important constituency. They used to hang out across the street at Gil's, which is now a cell phone shop. Back then, the Double Play seemed too hifalutin, said retired letter carrier George Hernandez, no relation to the owners.

"Gil's was blue-collar and this was more lawyers, cops, and politicians. I avoided this place like the plague because I didn't fit in. Right now I fit in."

Another letter carrier, Norma Jean, stops in on her way home most afternoons. She is the union boss of her postal branch and walks a grueling route in the Castro District. "I'm the safety officer at work and a lot more," she said. "I'm shop steward, shop physiologist, and shop sexologist. You know how many steps I got on my route? 1,298. And, I got 98 gates. No wonder I got bad knees."

Rafael Hernandez Jr.

Christina Hernan

If tears are flowing at the Double Play, animals are to blame as much as no-good boyfriends. Across Sixteenth Street, the SPCA generates bar business. Sometimes it's adopters dropping in for a celebratory shot. More often it's a sad occasion. On a recent morning a teary women walked in at 8:30 a.m. wearing a sweat suit and carrying a portable cat kennel. She said she had been up all night. She ordered a breakfast burrito, a diet Coke, and proceeded to drink two mai tais. "I just euthanized Sammy—she was an old lady," she said, pointing to the cat case. "She had a good run."

George Hernandez has lived a few blocks south of the Double Play, on Harrison Street, since 1944. As a retired postal worker, he has a government pension and owns his house. Everyone tells him he should cash out—the Mission is the hottest real estate in San Francisco. He doesn't care. Instead he tinkers around the house, goes by the Double Play for a beer or two, and reminisces about cheering on the Seals and the Giants in his youth. "Honestly, I never cared about the baseball—I only went for the hot dogs my cousin would buy me," he said. "I'm going to die on my block. After seventy-one years, you think I'm going to move out now? What am I going to do—sit in Modesto or Stockton looking around at my nice big house? All my friends are here."

THE CASTRO

TWIN PEAKS TAVERN, EST. 1972

401 Castro Street

Mary Ellen Cunha and Peggy Forster were not trying to make history in 1972 when they installed the full-length plate-glass windows at the Twin Peaks Tavern. They were trying to make a view. "People were used to being in windowless bars, but I didn't like it," Cunha told the San Francisco Planning Department in 2012. "We wanted to look out! We didn't want to sit in a bar and not be able to look out."

With the installation of those windows, the Twin Peaks Tavern became the first gay bar in the United States where patrons were clearly visible through open glass windows. And forty years later, the glass affords a dugout view of the most San Franciscan of junctions: where Castro Street dips to Market; where Seventeenth Street terminates; where nudists sit pocketless in the pocket park; where the historic F-line streetcar turns around; where protesters gather under the gay flag; where downtown workers transfer underground; where the basilica of movie palaces, the Castro Theatre, draws a thousand people for a *Sound of Music* sing-along one night and the same number for a drag spectacular featuring Peaches Christ in her silver-sequined *Charlie's Angels*-inspired jumpsuit the next.

"At some point everything that exists on earth walks by these windows, especially at 2:30 a.m." said current co-owner Jeff Green.

Osborne Bye and William Mullane opened Twin Peaks Tavern in 1935 and sold it to Robert Clancy after World War II. At the time, the neighborhood, then known as Eureka Valley, was a largely Irish enclave with smatterings of German and Scandinavian families. Holy Redeemer Church was the social center of the community. Eureka Valley had its own slogan: "the Sunny Heart of San Francisco." After World War II, families started to flee for the suburbs, making relatively cheap Victorian homes available to gays who had been scattered around

North Beach, Polk Street, SoMa, and other neighborhoods.

The bar Cunha and Forster bought had front windows that were painted black "so wives couldn't see their husbands drinking in here," said patron Matthew Wright, according to Moses Corrette who wrote a landmark designation report for the city's planning department.

In addition to opening up the western wall, Cunha and Forster, known as "the girls," ripped out the drop ceiling and converted a little office on the end into a mezzanine overlooking the bar. They added synchronized, flashing, arrow-shaped, rainbow-colored lights pointing to the entry. "We wanted to put out the gay-colored lights, but we couldn't find them anywhere, so we...painted them down in my basement," Forster said. "The sign was gorgeous! It still is. You can see it from Divisadero, or Market, or on the news."

Forster already had an interest some bars around town—the Mint, the Golden Cask, the Blue and Gold. The vibe at the Twin Peaks was genteel fussiness. It was a "fern bar" modeled after Henry Africa's at Polk and Broadway—brass fittings, antique tables and chairs, stained-glass lamps, hanging fern plants in the windows. Norman Hobday, inventor of the fern bar and proprietor of Henry Africa's, said he wanted to replace the "opium-den atmosphere" common at the time with "antique lamps and Grandma's living-room furniture." Twin Peaks was also a "don't touch" bar—patrons who made out were asked to go elsewhere. "Who wants to sit in a bar and watch people misbehave?" said Cunha.

The Castro was quickly becoming one of the most famous "gayborhoods" in the world—and the Twin Peaks was right in the middle of it. In 1972 San Francisco's gay population had reached 90,000, according to city health department estimates. By 1980 it was 120,000—18 percent of the city. Harvey Milk opened his camera shop in 1973 and would stop by for coffee. Twin Peaks regulars put together a marching band for the first "Gay Freedom Day" events, which evolved into the Pride parade. In 1974 the Twin Peaks softball team won the Gay Community Softball League, earning the right to face off against the SFPD Central Station team. They won. "Police Beaten!" the *New York Post* declared—and San Francisco Police Chief Donald Scott showed up outside the bar with sirens blaring to salute the team.

When Supervisor Dan White killed Milk and Mayor George Moscone at City Hall, and was subsequently acquitted, rioting erupted in the Civic Center and the Castro. Police raided the Elephant Walk, another Castro Bar, but not Twin Peaks, where bartenders lowered the lights and instructed patrons to lie on the floor as riot cops assembled at Market and Castro.

In the 1980s as the AIDS epidemic ravaged San Francisco's gay community, Twin Peaks became a de facto center for memorials and for fundraising. The bar remains in the top three for small businesses in the annual AIDS walk. "We must have lost ten or more bartenders....They were young healthy men and pretty soon their bodies [were] just gone," said Cuhna.

Regulars Neil Ostgaard and "Mayor Ed" Lee

Regular Jeremy Stadlberger

In 2001 "the girls" sold the bar to a pair of bartenders, Jeff Green and George Roeme. They've kept the place much the same: the old wooden bar, the no-food bar menu, and the music at a conversational level. "We were relieved when Jeff and George bought the bar; after all, it could have become a McDonald's," said Cuhna.

As many of the Castro's gay residents have reached retirement, the bar has been slapped with derisive nicknames like the Glass Coffin and Heaven's Waiting Room. But regulars say they don't really apply any more. Today, Twin Peaks is increasingly mixed—old/young, gay/straight, local/tourist—and is one of two San Francisco bars designated a historic landmark. Tourists stop in to ask directions and end up staying for a few hours. At the northern end of the bar, they often find "Mayor Ed" Lee sitting with an old friend, Neil Ostgaard.

"That's the biggest question: 'How do I get to Twin Peaks? What bus do I take?'" said Ostgaard, a Vietnam vet who was shot down twice in one day in Laos. "They look up Twin Peaks and end up here." Ostgaard and Mayor Ed have a repertoire of states songs for geographically appropriate interlopers. Minnesotans get "Ya oughta go ta Minnesota / see the cattle and the wheat / and the folks that can't be beat." Ohioans are greeted with: "What is round on the ends and high in the middle? It's O'hi'O."

"I tell you, we do have fun," said Ostgaard. "Anyone who is a tourist and goes to a bar doesn't go there to sit by themselves and sulk. They love it when someone says hi, and we do that all the time."

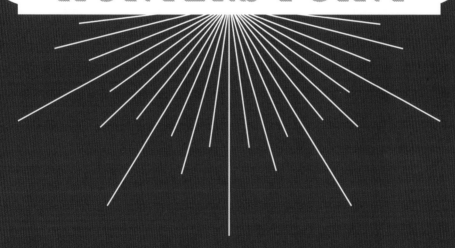

BAYVIEW–HUNTERS POINT

SILVER CREST DONUT SHOP, EST. 1970

340 Bayshore Boulevard

The Silver Crest never closes. It says so right above the door, spelled out in red neon: "We Never Close."

Nina and George Giavris bought the Silver Crest in 1970. Since that day they have never turned off the grill, never locked the door, never extinguished the fluorescent lights above the faux wood–paneled dining room. That's 16,500 days of donuts, over-easy eggs, and complimentary shots of ouzo, which is what you get if you venture into the dim back barroom and Nina decides you look all right.

The Silver Crest is a part roadhouse, part donut shop, part greasy spoon. The bar in back is separated by a wall and row of windows. Opened in 1895, the place started as a gas station and provisions store, serving traffic on what was then called the Old San Bruno Toll Road. It morphed into what it is today in the 1940s as manufacturers, printers, general contractors, and building materials suppliers staked their claims on what became Bayshore Boulevard, a congested 110-foot-wide, four-lane hodgepodge cutting between the industrial Bayview District and the freeway.

Nina and George came to San Francisco from Tripoli in November 1959. Nina worked at a laundry. George was a

mechanic at a factory. His crew used to go to the Silver Crest for a slice of pie and a cup of coffee. But work was unpredictable, and George thought he might prefer New York or Chicago. But Nina didn't want to leave San Francisco, so they looked around for a place to buy. "He wasn't supposed to be no restaurant owner," Nina said.

George and Nina didn't think the Silver Crest needed much in the way of improvement. They installed the interior windows between the bar and the diner. They moved the eight-stool bar from the east to the west wall. Aside from this, it has not changed since 1962, according to Edward "Fast Eddie" Pagan, who has been hanging out there since that year, when he was fifteen. "I remember when Nina bought the place. She was standing over there by the door with George, young and pretty."

At the time, Bayshore had more industry and a lot less fast food. Three miles down the road in Visitation Valley, more than a thousand workers manufactured metal locks at the Schlage Lock factory. In the 1970s, business was brisk enough that it took three waitresses to handle the crowds on the dining floor. The parking lot sparkled with the chrome and fins of big American cars. "They used to have pies and cakes lined up on the counter and the coffee was fifteen cents a cup," said Pagan.

But Bayshore Boulevard, dumping ground for garbage that most San Francisco neighborhoods would reject, gradually changed. In the 1980s, McDonald's, Jack in the Box, Domino's, and Burger King all built on land previously home to warehouses. Schlage Lock shut down in 1999. Goodman Lumber closed in 2005 and sat empty for five years until Lowe's built there.

Nina is still upset about all the fast food. "We tried to buy the lot across the street in 1983. We put money down. They don't give it to us—they give it to the McDonald for the fast food," she said. "Who knows what happened? They destroy it. Make it ugly. They bring the homeless people. It was all the working people down here."

Today, the Silver Crest is rarely busy, but its regulars are faithful. As a recent workday drew to a close, Alan Charles Clair III entered the bar. His boots were soggy from hanging scaffolding all day in the rain. He bowlegged it past the pool table with a limp. Al knows his way around a pool table. "Oh Mom, I am so tired," he told Nina. "Been up since five. Got to get out of these wet shoes."

Nina—everyone calls her Mom—sat hunched over on a stool in a purple turtleneck and shawl. She opened a bottle of Bud and poured Al's brandy shot. Al gets paid at the end of the month, and that's when he settles his bill. Nina knows everything about all her mostly male regulars: when their parents are in the hospital, how their grandkids are doing in school, when their ex-wives are giving them a hard time.

Al hits the Silver Crest twice a day, before work and after he gets off. When he jumps on a Greyhound to see his sick mom in Colorado, he makes sure to call and check in with his other mom at the Silver Crest. "It's my little spot," he said. "They treat me like I'm VIP, poor as I am. I ain't really poor. I'm just saying, Nina and George treat me well."

Nina is thoroughly unimpressed by the Silver Crest's history. She couldn't care less about the people who owned it before she and George took over. "It don't make no difference," she said. "The people died. You can't bring them back. What do I care about today? It's going to rain or not to rain." Nor is she interested in keeping up with the times. The TV in the corner doesn't work. Customers have the choice between one draft beer (Miller) and one bottled beer (Bud). They won't poach your eggs. They won't make you an omelet. The donuts are made twice a day.

The jukebox is 50 percent 1971, 50 percent 1984. That was the last time it was updated. Patti LaBelle meets New Kids on the Block. Six of the numbers are simply labeled "Greek Song." You can play three tracks for a quarter. Al says you can get four tracks if you know how to drop the coin in "just so." He doesn't have a quarter just now, but Chris Earley does. Chris is a carpenter by day and blues guitarist by night. He wears a porkpie hat and silver goatee. He stops by after work almost every day, splitting his time between his brother's couch in Bernal Heights and a pad in Nevada City. Like most regulars, Chris knows most of the jukebox by heart. He likes the Greek tunes because, he says, "those old Greeks pretty much downloaded the Persian scale."

"Give me a number," said Chris.

"U-3," said Al. "'I Love To See You Smile.' Bobby Blue Bland."

Regular Alan Charles Cla[...]

Regular Eddie Pa[...]

"I'll play it second. First up is L-2. 'Red Sails in the Sunset.'" It's by Tom Hall.

Al can carry a tune. "Red sails in the sunset way out to sea," he sang.

"It's 1974 all over again in here," said Chris.

"It's old-fashioned, but it works," said Al. "This ain't never gonna change. George and Nina will remain the same. That's one thing for sure."

Having a place that never closes is like having a friend that always has your back. Fast Eddie, sixty-six, is out on disability from his last job cleaning airplanes for Southwest Airlines. He spends most of his time taking care of his mother and worrying about his family. Eddie's sixteen-year old grandson has a kid on the way. "Babies having babies," he said.

"I come in here twelve o'clock at night, ten o'clock at night, three o'clock in the morning, and everybody in here knows me," said Eddie. "Don't have to worry about getting beat up because a lot of people in here are going to back me up." He looked around the mostly empty barroom. "Nina, how many people do I know over here?"

"You know too many," she said. "Everybody like you, Eddie."

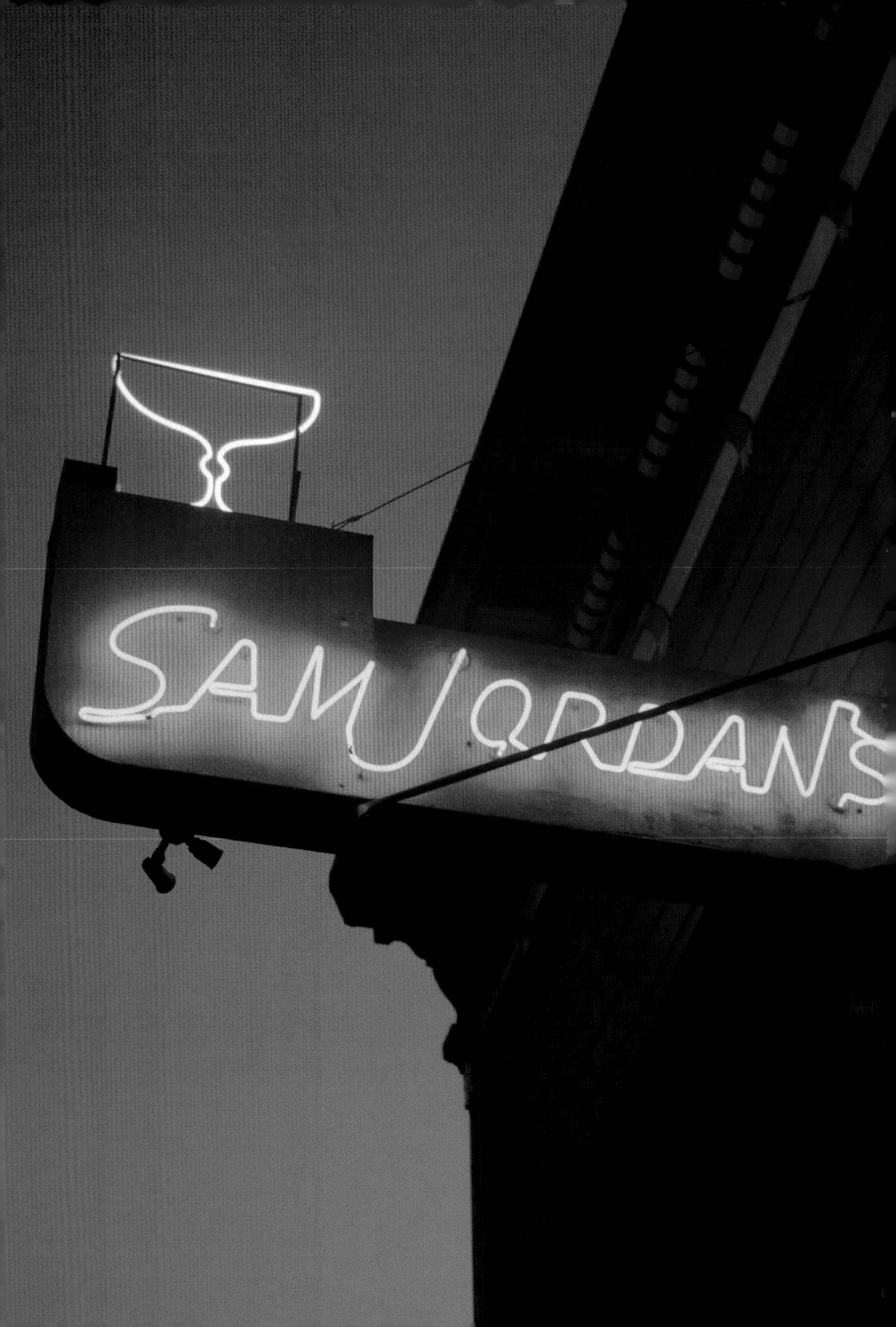
SAM JORDAN'S

SAM JORDAN'S BAR AND GRILL, EST. 1959

4004 Third Street

Sam Jordan sang when he worked. Sometimes it was "Blowin' in The Wind," the Stevie Wonder version, or Larry Graham's "One in a Million." His favorite song, his anthem, was Jay Jay Taylor's "I'm Not Tired Yet." He sang that song about every day—often to his wife, Bertha Ruth "Jenny" Jordan, a nurse who helped out at the bar.

> *"All the years I've been by your side*
> *Never once have I stopped to think about my pride*
> *I've been lovin' you a long time*
> *And I'm not tired yet."*

But how could he not have been tired? That's what his daughter, Ruth Jordan, wonders. Ruth runs the bar at Sam Jordan's; her brother Allen, the kitchen. Back in his day their dad, who died in 2003, smoked the brisket, fried the catfish, balanced the books, and catered everything from grammar school graduations to delegation parties at the 1984 Democratic Convention. His specialty was birthday cakes—he made a frosting portrait of the birthday celebrant with a little cutout for a champagne bottle.

In his spare time Sam Jordan was father to six kids, a champion Golden Gloves boxer, a mayoral candidate and, in the words of his friend Ed Flowers, a "one-man private foundation."

"I just don't get it," said Ruth Jordan. "He did everything. Just keeping on top of this bar drives me crazy."

Sam Jordan's is two-story, mint-green house of ribs and soul music in a part of town where the jobs remain dirty and hard. It abuts a construction yard piled high with old paint buckets, lumber, and HVAC ducts. On the same block is a forklift leasing company, a mattress distributor, and an autobody shop. Around the corner is the Southeast Wastewater Treatment Plant. Sam's serves up a contrast: walking down the block on warm fall evenings you can hear the funk and smell the fried chicken, the recipe for which a young white blogger recently asked Allen Jordan.

Jordan paused for a couple of seconds. "Salt and pepper," he said. "And *black power.*"

Sam Jordan, born in 1925 in the sawmill town of Diboll, Texas, arrived in San Francisco at age twenty-two, one of tens of thousands of African American military veterans to head west during and after the war for jobs in Bay Area shipyards. Between 1940 and 1950, San Francisco's African American population climbed 900 percent, from 5,000 to 43,000. Jordan lived on Double Rock Road in shoddy housing that had been thrown together for war-industry employees at the Hunters Point Shipyard. Like most of the men on Double Rock, he was a waterfront guy all the way—International Longshore and Warehouse Union.

He was also a go-getter. In the boxing ring he was Singing Sam, known for belting out "The Star-Spangled Banner" after belting his opponent into submission. He started janitorial and catering businesses. He was a "nose to the grindstone guy with good ideas," said Flowers. "Was he chairman of the board at General Motors? No. But he did a lot of different things."

By 1958 Jordan had saved enough money to buy 4004 Third Street, an 1883 Italianate with a bar on the first story and an apartment upstairs. At the time it was Lagrave's Tavern, a gathering place for men largely working in the animal processing trades, which dominated the district then known as Butchertown. Jordan changed the name and turned it into more of a cocktail lounge with booths along the wall and a horseshoe-shaped stage in the back where the kitchen is today. "Sam Jordan's" was spelled out above the door in red cursive neon. Big Mama Thornton stopped by often, as did four-foot-eleven soul dynamo Sugar Pie DeSanto, who lived nearby on Williams Street. The bar drew employees from the shipyards as well as the Allen Meatpacking Plant, located at Third and Evans, the last of the rendering plants in the neighborhood. Sam became known as the Mayor of Butchertown.

"Sam cashed the checks for most of the guys," said Joe Hill, who drove a delivery truck for 7UP, then down the street from Sam's on Yosemite. "This bar wasn't about no youngsters. This bar was about OGs. The gentlemen used to come in here with the suits and hats and the ladies had on their mink coats. When they got up to dance they left their furs at the table and nobody walked away with them. It was the classiest place on Third Street."

Sam Jordan lived by the adage that charity begins at home. To that he might have added: not behind the bar. Never a drinker himself, when it came to dispensing alcohol he was a heavyweight champ who served featherweight drinks. "If Sam was pouring you were going to get nothing more than a regulated shot," said Ruth.

Food was a different matter. Sam kept a table next to the kitchen for folks who were down on their luck. "If he was cookin', you was welcome," said Ruth. "Allen does the same thing."

"Yup," said Allen. "I might not give you a couple of dollars to let you go do what you've got no business doing, but I'll feed you."

Sam Jordan was a civil rights crusader who favored dashikis and wooden African necklaces. The bar was a Butchertown think tank—ideas that came out of Sam Jordan's included a neighborhood-based food panty, an African American merchants association, and a senior theater troupe. His signature dish was "African Corn"—sweet corn mixed with ground beef and spices. The dish remains the Jordan family calling card. "People always ask, 'Why did your daddy call it African Corn?' I say, 'He was Afrocentric. Anything he would do was African,'" said Ruth. "If he fried eggs, they were African eggs."

In 1963 Sam Jordan was the first African American to run for mayor, finishing fourth in a field of eight. After that, he

Regulars Vincent and Robyn

Allen Jordan, Ruth Jordan, and Sam Jordan Jr.

served as a neighborhood ward healer, confidante of politicians ranging from U.S. Senator Dianne Feinstein to former mayors Willie Brown and Frank Jordan. If you were laid off or between opportunities, you'd end up on Sam Jordan's payroll, according to Bill Scott, who worked for Jordan. "When you were around Sam, you know what you were in danger of? Having something nice done to you by Sam," he said. "That was your danger."

It has been a challenging few years for African Americans in the Bayview–Hunters Point District, a neighborhood in which 39 percent of families live below the poverty line. Between 1990 and 2010 San Francisco's African American population fell 36 percent, by nearly 30,000, as families left for cheaper suburbs like Antioch, Tracy, and Vallejo. In 2010, 58 percent of San Francisco's foreclosures were in the area.

Still, Bayview–Hunters Point remains a cultural and spiritual center for thousands of African American families in the Bay Area. And so does Sam's. At Sam's you meet a lot of people who came back to the old neighborhood after stints elsewhere. Others keep one foot in the Bayview and one in the East Bay, returning for church, work, or to care for an elderly relative. "Everyone you see here is the child, grandchild, or great grandchild of someone who was here originally," said Ron Booker, who has been going to Sam's since 1965. Asked if Sam Jordan would be surprised that the place is still open, Booker said, "Sam would love it because his kids are doing right with what he left them."

During happy hour, regulars retreat to the concrete back patio with its rickety tables and mismatched chairs. That's where the ribs are smoked and dance parties break out. Joe Hill, a retired truck driver, usually has a dominos or chess game going.

Jade Williams says Sam Jordan's "is like San Francisco weather." With the right rhythm section, the mood of the place can change between the opening verse and the chorus. Williams prays Sunday mornings at the New Mount Vernon Missionary Baptist Church and later heads to Sam's for karaoke night. Her go-to songs are Erykah Badu's "Tyrone" and Deborah Cox's "Nobody's Supposed to Be Here."

Sam's is the best karaoke in the city, Williams says. "People who should be famous, and people who shouldn't sing in the shower. I sing until the lights come on. If you don't want to have a good time, don't come here, because this is fun and family."

DOGPATCH

THE RAMP
BAR & RESTAURANT
855 CHINA BASIN

RUBY
SAILING

EMBARCADERO
**Rowing
Club**
www.RowRenegade.org

PUBLIC
SHORE

THE RAMP, EST. 1950

855 Terry A. Francois Boulevard

First came the boats and bait. Then the booze and burgers. That's the story of the Ramp.

In the early 1980s, San Francisco entrepreneur Mike Denman toured the boatyard in China Basin. With Southern Pacific's abandoned railroad yards due north and Pier 70's fading shipyards to the south, the boatyard was in its final throes. Its lease with the Port of San Francisco was expiring.

Denman loved the boatyard, but something intrigued him just as much as the potential he saw in the marine repair business. Next to the boatyard, beyond a dirt lane running down to a concrete ramp, was a bait shack with an improvised snack bar. It was a place where a sport fisherman could grab a bite, a beer, and a bag of anchovies and launch his vessel from Pier 66. The place had grit, gulls, and fish guts. It felt like part of a central waterfront that, even then, was vanishing from San Francisco.

"Somebody probably put in a hot dog machine. Somebody else put in a hamburger grill, and it evolved over time as a waterfront dive," Denman told *Bay Crossings* trade publication in 2001.

In 1983 Denman signed a short-term lease for the boatyard, which he renamed San Francisco Boat Works. A year later he took over the Ramp next door. He built a proper kitchen and a

small indoor bar with a handful of tables. Most of the seating remained where the original bait shack was, on the concrete patio overlooking the bay. Denman called it "the last of the old joints." "It's still a waterfront dive, just a little cleaned up and a little expanded," he explained at the time.

By the 1980s the industrial Dogpatch neighborhood had been in decline for decades. After World War II, jobs dried up at the Pier 70 shipyard. The Western Sugar Refinery moved overseas, as did Tubbs Cordage Company. From 1965 to 1980 the number of jobs in the central waterfront area, which includes Dogpatch, dropped from 16,304 to 11,004. Most of the losses occurred in manufacturing and ship repair.

At the same time, within Third Street's industrial warehouses and Dogpatch's 1880s Victorians was the spark of something new. Artists and architects started moving into buildings like the American Can Company. Urban homesteaders fixed up the Victorian workers' cottages on Minnesota and Tennessee Streets. Down on the decaying waterfront, hippies were restoring old wooden boats and taking up residence in houseboats on Mission Creek.

Joan Robins stumbled upon the Ramp in 1987. At the time, Robins, who had run restaurants in New York, was living on a boat in the creek and hanging out with salts and artists along the waterfront. When she walked down between the boatyard and the restaurant she saw Denman bent over, sweeping the patio. "I said, 'Wow, I've got to run this place,'" she recalled. Six months later she was running it. She has been running it ever since.

The Ramp is the only bar in San Francisco where the Saturday launch of a historic cutter can be as much a cause for celebration as a 49ers playoff win. On a Saturday morning in May of 2013, the champagne was flowing at San Francisco Boatworks as Allen Gross launched the *Folly,* an 1889 cutter—the "hot rod of her day." He had spent eight years restoring her. Before the boat was lowered into the bay, Gross called Denman "the soul of the waterfront" and thanked him, and the Ramp, for making the project possible. "You fed me like one of the staff," he said.

Robins and Denman operate the Ramp as carefully as Gross does his *Folly.* "It has been keeping it waterfront, keeping it natural, keeping it comfortable. And funky, funky, funky," Robins said. "You can get all the fancy stuff all over the city. Anywhere now. Anywhere. We do not want to become that because we have something different to offer."

The Ramp rocks, too. Robins has a deep appreciation of blues, soul, and especially Latin music. On any given Sunday afternoon, Cesar's Latin All Stars band might be jamming as Brazilian Cumbia dancers do their thing on the concrete patio and seagulls steal french fries from the dancers' temporarily abandoned lunches.

The rest of the week, the crowd is as diverse as any place in the city. In addition to boatyard workers and owners like Gross, you might get retired cops, prosecutors from the district attorney's office, and engineers from Airbnb down at the old Jewelry Mart building. The Carpenters Union is nearby, so those guys drop in. When the mega-cruise ships come and go from Pier 70, where they are repaired, the workers retire to the Ramp.

These days San Francisco's waterfront is attracting star chefs like Michael Chiarello and Charles Phan. All around the Ramp, Dogpatch is gentrifying furiously with new restaurants and condos. Corrine Woods, who lives on a houseboat in Mission Creek, said the community has had to fight to keep the boatyard and the Ramp from development.

One devoted Ramp regular is the Greek impresario Christo Kasaris, who has owned San Francisco restaurants like Samos Greek Restaurant and Bay City Bar and Grill. Nowadays Kasaris, who has a self-storage facility in Dogpatch, wonders if the Ramp will survive.

"A lot of us are getting squeezed out of here because new opportunities are coming in," he said. "The port wants new businesses. I think we should retain some of the beauty of San Francisco, a casual place like this that has existed for many years on the waterfront."

Kasaris was close to a longtime bartender of the Ramp, Al Poole, who's now retired in Panama. Poole lived on a boat and kept a skiff tied up below the Ramp. When a dinghy broke away from the dock, he would rescue it. Kasaris recalls the afternoon a regular caught a thirty-pound halibut and brought it back to the bar. "They had a barbecue going, so we cut it into fillets and cooked it up," said Kasaris. "Fresh fish, and good wine, and good friends. That's about it, right?"

BERNAL HEIGHTS

THE WILD SIDE WEST, EST. 1962

424 Cortland Avenue

When Gwen "Sugar Mama" Avery died unexpectedly in March of 2014, Wild Side West owner Billie Hayes went to work. Hayes had no doubt that the Wild Side West would host a memorial service for the Northern California blues singer, whose "Lesbian Concentrate" anthems were in heavy jukebox rotation at the Bernal Heights bar, and who could be found on occasion hunched over the bar's upright piano playing "Sugar in My Bowl." The only question was when.

On a rainy afternoon in late March, the pool table became a banquet table with a spread of sandwiches, meatballs, and potato salad. The piano was adorned with roses. Pictures chronicling Avery's life covered the walls. Roddy McCarthy stood in front of the brick fireplace and played "What a Wonderful Life" on his National steel guitar. Playwright Terry Baum shared a clip from a documentary she is making about Avery. Poet Clea Poetnoise King led the packed barroom in a chorus of growls, stomps, and refrains from "Sugar Mama," Avery's best-known song.

"We are here where Gwen Avery cut her teeth so many times," said King. "Drank her beer and wine. Talked real loud and stomped her feet and said 'I am here. Here I be.' Sugar Mama Done Gone. Sugar, Sugar, Sugar. Sugaaaaa Mamaaaaa."

There may not be a bar in San Francisco as deeply entwined with its surrounding neighborhood as the Wild Side West. It is a salon and a saloon, a neighborhood front parlor. It is part campfire song circle, part pool hall, part boardroom for the fringes of San Francisco politics. If the Wild Side West had a motto, it would be something that the bar's founder, the late Pat Ramseyer, could often be heard saying: "What are all these people doing in my living room?"

Ramseyer and partner Nancy White, both out lesbians, opened the bar in 1962 in Oakland. It was called the Wild Side after the Barbara Stanwyck film *Walk on the Wild Side*. Two years later they moved the party to Broadway in San Francisco's North Beach, which had not yet been consumed by topless clubs. There, "west" was added to "wild side," and the bar became the Wild Side West. Nancy was an attorney with business sense. Pat was an artist with charisma, a percussionist with the Berkeley electric band Bebe L'Roach. Her presence drew musicians like Jae Whitaker and Janice Joplin, who is said to have used the pool table (the same one in the bar today) for more strenuous activities than 8 Ball.

Finally, in 1976 the bar relocated to Bernal Heights, then a mostly Catholic working-class family neighborhood. To say the reception was less than warm would be an understatement. The bar had been open only a few days when someone strolled in and fired a gun at the ceiling. Old toilets and sinks were dumped overnight in front of the bar. Pat and Nancy were not deterred. "Pat said 'I'm not going—but thank you for the planters,'" said Hayes. "That is how the porcelain garden started."

Clea Poetnoise King

Owner Billie Hayes

Today, calla lilies grow in a claw-foot bathtub; succulents sprout from a urinal. The sign says "Welcome to Pat's Magical Garden." Around every corner there are swinging chairs, wrought-iron benches, stone lanterns, a robot built from Pabst Blue Ribbon cans. The aroma of pot mixes with jasmine in the springtime. Most Wild Side West regulars seem to have met their partners in the bar's rambling beer gardens.

Both Pat and Nancy have died. Billie Hayes, who was bequeathed the bar in Pat's will, says the Wild Side West was really a canvas for Pat's restless creativity, and she is trying to keep it that way. Pat is the bar's patron saint. Her paintings adorn the walls and a photograph of her hangs by her favorite spot at the north end of the bar, where a single rose sits in her memory. "She was electrifying. She could look at your soul and know who you were," said Hayes.

Pat could be both sweet and ornery. "You would go to leave the bar, she would say, 'Get back in here. You're not done yet. Come talk to me,'" recalled regular Kris. "If it got too quiet she would say 'Somebody play the goddamn jukebox.' If somebody fell down she would say 'What are you doing down there—get up and have a drink.'"

Baum, a playwright and Green Party activist, said the Wild Side West was where she had cast parties for all her plays. When Baum bucked the city's mainstream establishment by running for Congress, it was back to the Wild Side West. "Nobody would have a benefit for me because I was running against Nancy Pelosi. People who had volunteered ended up chickening out. It was really just the Wild Side that did it. It was the only place."

Kris, who works with the mentally ill on the streets of San Francisco, said that her generation is fading from the Wild Side West. Some have moved back east to care for elderly parents. Many have died. Other have retired and moved to the North Bay.

"They would come to see Pat. It was like moths to light," said Kris. "It was dykes galore all the time. Motorcycle women who would ride their bikes in the bar. A lot of us didn't have mothers to go to. She was like a mother to a lot of us. She would dig in, very private, but very good conversations."

At Pat's memorial service in 2012, state assembly member Tom Ammiano, a longtime Bernal Heights resident, said the Wild Side West changed Cortland Street and Bernal Heights. "It was not very gay friendly in those early days—it was not very friendly at all," he said. "I had to hit a lot of people with my purse getting up here. We have all paid a lot of dues. We survived with the spirit and magic of Pat."

Hayes, who cared for Pat during her final days, said she didn't have any idea she would be given the bar. And she doesn't want to change much. "If a tragedy happens, people meet here that same night or the next day. Everybody comes here. They know. You don't have to put out an announcement," Billie said. "They know they've got to come here."

WEST PORTAL

PHILOSOPHERS CLUB,
EST. 1960
824 Ulloa Street

The trouble with writing about a bar called the Philosophers Club is that one is tempted to include "philosopher walked into a bar" jokes, such as the one where a philosopher walks into a bar and orders a "Nietzschean beverage," to which the bartender says: "Sorry, Kant."

In truth, a philosopher did walk into the Philosophers Club a few years ago. His name was Jacob Needleman. He had taught philosophy at San Francisco State University for fifty years. He was at the bar in 2010 for the unveiling of a mural, by co-owner Deborah Sullivan, in which the portraits of fifty great thinkers are depicted on the barroom ceiling. Jean-Paul Sartre made the cut. So did Mother Theresa, John Lennon, Plato, Socrates, and Jacob Needleman.

It's the Sistine Chapel of San Francisco neighborhood watering holes. As the only deep-thinking celebrity with a local zip code, Needleman got a free drink. "It enchanted me to see my face up there next to the immortals," he said. "It was a curious honor. I was very touched by it. I felt at home there. I got a warm reception. I felt immortalized in a very local way, though it did make me feel a little like I was already dead."

To understand the Philosophers Club, which regulars call the Philly, you have to understand West Portal. And more than any other commercial center in San Francisco, it's a place defined by public infrastructure and mass transit. The portal in West Portal is the western terminal of a 2.3-mile tunnel that starts by the foot of the California Street office high-rise canyon and ends in a fragrant, foggy lushness west of Twin Peaks. The tunnel opened in 1918. At the time, builders had already started constructing fine single-family homes west of the peaks in St. Francis Wood and Forest Hill—a mix of Craftsman, prairie-style, Beaux-Arts and other styles. But they

Owners Dick and Tommy Donahue and family

didn't sell very well because the steep terrain separating the residential enclaves from jobs and entertainment made living there unpractical.

The tunnel connecting West of Twin Peaks to the city changed that. West Portal Avenue became the hub of commerce for areas like Ingleside Terraces, Sunnyside, Balboa Terrace, Forest Hill, and St. Francis Wood. It was a streetcar suburb popular with district attorneys, police brass, construction guys, nurses, teachers, upper-echelon bureaucrats, school administrators. It supplied parishioners with a trio of Catholic churches: St. Brendan, St. Cecilia, and St. Stephen. It had, and still has, its own movie theater, hardware store, diners, restaurants, bookstore, and bars.

The Philosophers Club opened in the 1930s after Prohibition. Before that, it was a dry-goods store serving the "sand hogs" assigned to the tunnel project.

Angelo d'George bought the bar in 1960 and ran it for forty-three years. Under his stewardship the Philly Club was a card room and, like a lot of bars back then, it would not have been impossible to place a bet on a ballgame. Angelo worked all the shifts himself. "He wore a red vest and poured wine out of a gallon jug," said Dick Donahue, co-owner of the bar today. "To turn the heat on he would put two wires together. Mixed drinks were served in little juice glasses. He always had a game of cards in the back. He took care of a lot of people, he cooked a lot, he made sure people ate. He took care of business, but he also had a heart."

The place had a drop ceiling and slits for windows. "This was a dark cave; you didn't know if it was two in the afternoon or two in the morning," Donahue said. "The customers ran tabs. They would shake dice for absolutely everything. They would shake dice to see who could go the bathroom."

Current owners Dick and Tommy Donahue, who are brothers, grew up three blocks from the bar, and Deb Sullivan was raised in nearby Forest Knolls. Her husband, Sully, grew up in Boston and Buffalo and played football at Dartmouth College.

The Donahues first tried to buy a place in the neighborhood in 1980, the Forest Club (now McCarthy's), but the deal went sideways, so they bought the Marina Lounge instead. There they employed a bartender named Sully and befriended his wife, Deborah, who had been a bartender at the Washington Square Bar and Grill.

"West Portal is the only district in the city that has maintained its culture throughout time," said Dick Donahue. "There are still a lot parents and grandparents living in the homes they grew up in through the thirties and forties and fifties. When people here ask where you went to school, they are talking about grammar school, not college."

The row of football helmets on a shelf above the back bar reveal some of the bar's preoccupations. There is St. Ignatius (where the Donahues went), Sacred Heart, Riordan, Lincoln High School, Cal, and Stanford. There is a police helmet donated by regular Greg Corrales, retired captain from Mission Station. High school sports are big at the Philly. "We have to keep the napkins behind the bar or all those high school coaches will use them up mapping out plays," said Donahue.

The philosophical discourse at the Philly Club is more likely to involve defensive formations than epistemology. But Deborah Sullivan, who has a degree in fine arts, decided that she would paint a mural that gives some meaning to the bar's name. She sat in on one of Needleman's classes at San Francisco State—"it was about something called the fifth dimension"—and in a binder she compiled quotes and biographical information about each luminary thinker depicted in the mural. She keeps it behind the bar and pulls it out when patrons express interest in the mural. "I wanted somebody from every culture, ethnicity," said Sullivan, looking through the book. "Here is Joseph Campbell—his philosophy is follow your bliss and you will feel like you never worked a day in your life. Wouldn't that be nice?"

Needleman said he is looking for an excuse to visit the bar, and the mural, again. "I'm looking for an opportunity to impress my friends, or maybe my daughter—I'd like to impress her," he said. "More good philosophizing is done in bars than anywhere else—and I'm only half joking."

FISHERMAN'S WHARF

NORTH BEACH

MARINA

RUSSIAN HILL

CHINATOWN

FINANCIAL DIST.

PACIFIC HEIGHTS

NOB HILL

PRESIDIO

UNION SQ.

TENDERLOIN

PRESIDIO HEIGHTS

CIVIC CENTER

SEA CLIFF

WESTERN ADDITION / JAPANTOWN

SOMA / SOUTH BEACH

RICHMOND

HAYES VALLEY

HAIGHT-ASHBURY

GOLDEN GATE PARK

INNER SUNSET

CASTRO

MISSION

POTRERO HILL

DOGPATCH

SUNSET

TWIN PEAKS

NOE VALLEY

DIAMOND HEIGHTS

BERNAL HEIGHTS

PARKSIDE

GLEN PARK

WESTWOOD HIGHLANDS

BAYVIEW

BALBOA TERRACE

PORTOLA

HUNTERS POINT

LAKESHORE

INGLESIDE

EXCELSIOR

OCEANVIEW

CROCKER-AMAZON

VISITACION VALLEY

N

W

S

HAIGHT-ASHBURY

AUB ZAM ZAM, EST. 1942

1633 Haight Street

Looking back, David Gutekunst thinks he was lucky Bruno didn't throw him out when he walked into the Zam Zam in 1985. Gutekunst was dusty after hanging Sheetrock all day in a building around the corner. He was joking around with his colleague, thirsty and boisterous after ten hours of noisy work.

Perhaps Bruno was in a charitable mood. Or he took pity on a couple of guys covered in plaster powder and paint chips. Bruno liked hard workers. Whatever the reason, he didn't do what he usually did when customers fell short of his exacting code of decorum. He didn't suggest that Gutekunst would find "the corner bar" more appealing. Instead, Bruno simply said, "Gentlemen, *please*, a little *pianissimo.*" He took their order.

Gutekunst was impressed. Who was this short, plump character in a vest, tie, and cuff-linked monogrammed shirt on the boulevard of beads, bongs, and runaway hippies? "I didn't know the whole rigmarole about Bruno," said Gutekunst.

The rigmarole about Bruno: it's still on the menu at the Zam Zam thirty years later. Bruno died in 2000, but at some point most afternoons the discussion at the small semicircular bar circles back to the myth of Bruno Mooshei, the crusty contrarian who became a Haight-Ashbury icon by railing against the very peace, drugs, and rock 'n' roll the neighborhood was famous for. "You come through these doors and it's as if he passed away yesterday," said bartender Joseph Tessitore.

Bartender Kandar Baidwan

Bruno was born in in 1920 in Baghdad as his Assyrian parents were en route to the United States from what is now Northern Iran. Arriving in San Francisco, the family settled in a flat on the corner of Haight and Ashbury Streets, opening a five-stool greasy spoon called the Pall Mall. By 1941, by then well established in the city, Bruno's father, Sam Mooshei, opened the Persian Zam Zam at 1933 Haight Street. He hired Jon Oshanna, a fellow Assyrian, to design an exterior with decorative Moorish archways and twin minarets, and an interior mural on canvas depicting the tragic love story of King Khosrow and Princess Shirin. "It was Sam trying to build a perfect little shrine to what he loved about Bagdad," said Zam Zam bartender Kandar Baidwan.

The Haight Street that Bruno grew up on felt like a village tucked between Golden Gate Park and Buena Vista Park. Shopkeepers knew one another. Streetcars staggered up Haight Street to Golden Gate Park. The neighborhood had two of the city's marquee high schools: Lowell, then located at Hayes and Masonic Streets, and Polytechnic, where Bruno went. The Poly-Lowell football game on Thanksgiving regularly drew ten thousand fans to Kezar Stadium. In the afternoon after school, Bruno swept the floor at the Pall Mall and waited on bookies who took wagers in the basement. Once, Bruno found a ten-dollar bill a gambler had dropped on the stairs. He celebrated by taking friends to the soda fountain.

After high school, Bruno joined the United States Navy as a medic and was assigned to the marines at Guadalcanal.

When he got home, he worked for the City of San Francisco in the pension department for a couple of years before joining his father's business. He took over the Zam Zam in 1951.

The Zam Zam stood out, not just because of its Middle Eastern flair, but because it was the classiest cocktail lounge on Haight Street. The forties and fifties would remain, for Bruno, San Francisco's golden era. He liked "sweet music" or "hotel society music" like Carmen Cavallaro, Leo Reisman's Orchestra, and Ray Noble. "He hated the sound of the human voice," said Gutekunst.

If there was a golden era on Haight Street at that time, it was fast vanishing. Families were packing up for the suburbs and the Avenues. Investors were picking up Queen Anne Victorians and chopping them up into rooming houses for students and artists. The Beat era had faded and the Haight was replacing North Beach as the center of San Francisco counterculture. Most historians argue that the hippies brought new energy to the Haight-Ashbury. Not Bruno. "He was appalled by the hippies," said Bob Clarke, who now owns the bar. "Business was decimated."

The crazier Haight Street got, the fussier Mooshei became. Women got napkins; men did not. A martini was served in a chilled three-ounce glass. It was made with Boord's gin and Boissiere vermouth in a ratio, he often said, of a thousand to one. Upon entering the Zam Zam a customer was to do three things: sit at a stool, put their money on the bar, and order a proper drink. A beer was not a proper drink.

If a group of newly arrived patrons deliberated too long, Bruno would stand, smoke, and watch them. Finally, when they were ready, he would say, "I came over here to try to give you good service, but you refused it. So why don't you go to the corner bar. You'll like the corner bar. They have young bartenders. They have beards."

"You came in with money and a purpose—you didn't stare like a flycatcher with your mouth open," said Baidwan.

Bruno became famous for saying no and tossing people out of the bar. His truculence was the subject of a 4,200-word essay in the *London Review of Books* by poet August Kleinzahler. One day a producer from *Late Night with David Letterman* called to see if the talk show host could be thrown out of the Zam Zam. Bruno was not impressed. "Who is this David Letterman?" he asked the regulars. "I don't know this person. Why do these people bother me? He must be some New York person." Bruno hated New York; he didn't like anything east of Reno.

When he was behind the bar, Bruno drank "old tennis shoes"—a shot of bourbon. He called them "shotskis." He smoked Pall Malls unfiltered. Bruno worked four nights a week. When he didn't feel like working, he simply didn't open the bar. He was a dues-paying member of Local 2, the hotel and restaurant union, but never had a boss, never mind an employee. On Sundays Bruno and his pals would go out for steaks. They hit Cattlemens in Santa Rosa and Flames in San Jose. When he went to Reno he called it "going on strike."

Bruno died of prostate cancer in 2000 at age eighty. Before he passed away he sold the bar to Clarke, a regular who lived upstairs. Clarke hired art-restoration specialist Ann Rosenthal to clean up the mural. "It took her three days to dig through the layers of nicotine," said Clarke. "I just felt fortunate to be able to preserve as much as possible a piece of San Francisco history."

To mark the bar's fortieth anniversary in 1983, one of the Zam Zam regulars put together a promotional pamphlet. It laid out the narrative of the Haight-Ashbury, as Bruno saw it:

"Life was simple" until the "sinful sixties" arrived. "Some of the villagers were able to seek refuge in Bruno's establishment. While the marauders marched down Haight Street, Bruno cut slices of lemon peel and pierced olives with golden toothpicks."

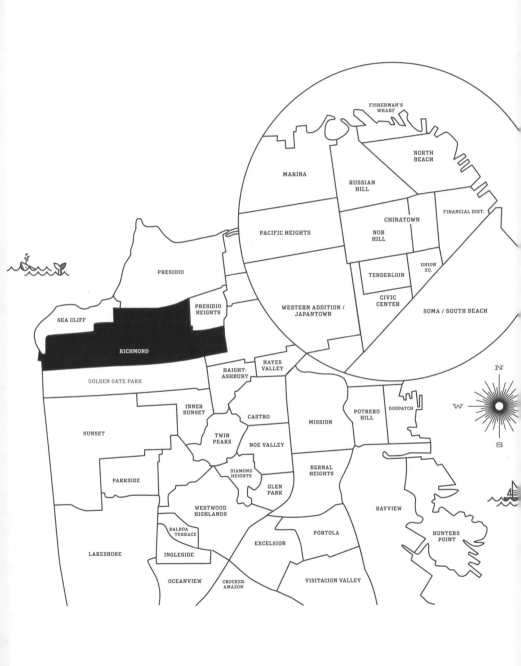

FISHERMAN'S
WHARF

NORTH
BEACH

MARINA

RUSSIAN
HILL

FINANCIAL DIST.

CHINATOWN

PACIFIC HEIGHTS

NOB
HILL

PRESIDIO

UNION
SQ.

PRESIDIO
HEIGHTS

TENDERLOIN

SEA CLIFF

CIVIC
CENTER

SOMA / SOUTH BEACH

WESTERN ADDITION /
JAPANTOWN

RICHMOND

GOLDEN GATE PARK

HAYES
VALLEY

HAIGHT-
ASHBURY

INNER
SUNSET

CASTRO

MISSION

POTRERO
HILL

DOGPATCH

SUNSET

TWIN
PEAKS

NOE VALLEY

N

W

DIAMOND
HEIGHTS

BERNAL
HEIGHTS

S

PARKSIDE

GLEN
PARK

WESTWOOD
HIGHLANDS

BAYVIEW

BALBOA
TERRACE

PORTOLA

HUNTERS
POINT

LAKESHORE

INGLESIDE

EXCELSIOR

OCEANVIEW

CROCKER-
AMAZON

VISITACION VALLEY

THE RICHMOND

TRAD'R SAM, est. 1937

6150 Geary Boulevard

Dorothy Munguia Riedel has never touched the stuff herself, but that's never stopped her from concocting some of the most potent tropical cocktails between Tahiti and Haight-Ashbury. For thirty-seven years the Greek American matriarch has presided over Trad'r Sam, arguably the oldest "bamboo bar" in the United States. A remnant of a 1930s-era Polynesian Pop craze that has mostly vanished, Sam's is a wheel of rattan booths rotating from a six-blender horseshoe bar. And if the whole place seems to be spinning, blame Dorothy. "She made everything taste like candy," said daughter Angie Munguia, who worked at the bar along with her brother, sister, uncle, and cousin.

Trad'r Sam opened in 1937 with the motto "Home of the Banana Cow." The Top Banana was Sam Baden. He was surfing a cocktail wave pioneered down south by Don Beach, who had struck gold with the concept at Don the Beachcomber in Hollywood.

The music came first. The 1937 Bing Crosby musical *Waikiki Wedding* introduced songs like "Sweet Leilani" and "Little Hula Heaven." A generation of teenagers started picking up ukuleles and slack-key guitars. Club owners caught on, booking Hawaiian acts and tricking out their venues with rattan mats, fishing-net floats, bamboo-cladded walls, and murals of cavorting islanders.

Owner Dorothy Munguia Reidel with daughters Angie and Helen, and neice Joanne

Trad'r Sam remained the city's sole Polynesian-themed bar during World War II, according to Chris VerPlanck, who wrote a report on tiki bars for the city's Historic Preservation Commission. After the war it was joined by the Tonga Room, which opened in 1945 in the Fairmont Hotel, the Bamboo Hut on Broadway, Trader Jay Jay on Polk Street, the Hilo Hut on Larkin Street, and the Tahitian Hut on Geary Street.

A new wave of tiki bars crashed on San Francisco's shores in the mid-1950s: the Aloha Club, the Hawaiian Village, the Mauna Loa, Pago Pago, Trader's Village, Skipper Kent's, and Tiki Bob's. And the most famous tiki impresario of all, Victor Jules Bergeron, opened his first Trader Vic's venue in Oakland, eventually adding twenty-four more around the globe.

Tiki bars in San Francisco began disappearing during the late 1960s and early 1970s as the portrayal of islanders as frolicking, exotic creatures began to feel condescending and exploitative. By 1980, there was only a handful listed in the city directories, and by 1995 only three remained: the Tonga Room, Trad'r Sam, and the Marina District's Mauna Loa, which, while Hawaiian owned, never played up the Polynesian/tiki themes.

Baden eventually passed Trad'r Sam on to Doug Montgomery, who in turn sold it in 1978 to the Munguias, a Greek American bar-owning family rooted in the Mission District. It was a perfect Richmond District story. Greeks from the Mission making Polynesian cocktails in a neighborhood dominated by Irish, Chinese, and Russians.

The Munguias never felt the need to change the already fifty-year-old décor. They retained the lauhala mat soffit above the bar. The names of South Sea Islands are still spelled out in bamboo at the entrance to each booth. Dorothy did update the drink menu, however. The P-38—it has "almost every shot in the well"—was too heavy on the crème de menthe. The Black Magic was pink, the color of Pepto-Bismol. "It's Black Magic—it should be a dark color, right? I rearranged that whole drink," she said.

She created the King Louis in her father's honor: amoretto, vanilla ice cream, rum, and whipped cream. The Volcano came in a fish bowl and featured a few rums, vodka, grenadine, and orange sherbet. It erupted in orange foam. "People always

want the recipes," said Dorothy. "I would tell then what's in it, but I would always leave out a few things."

Eventually, Dorothy's daughter Helen and niece Joanne started working as cocktail waitresses. Her daughter Angie and son Demo took over behind the bar. Angie studied her mom's techniques. She met two husbands and more than one or two boyfriends at the bar. Her first husband, who was French, came in with a group of neighborhood Chinese kids. They were twenty-one. The French guy was twenty. "He was underage so I kicked him out," Angie said of her former husband. "He used to stand outside the bar and wait for me until I got off."

The bar has always hosted an older crowd of locals in the afternoon and on weeknights, with students pouring in on weekend nights. It is an eclectic mix characteristic of the Richmond District, with a heavy representation from Irish construction trades. "The fights would start in here and we would manage to get them all outside," recalled Dorothy. "One time I called the cops and told 'em 'There's a huge fight in front of Trad'r Sam. They asked, 'Well, tell me, what nationality are they?' I said, 'What nationality? Are you kidding me? It's international! You name it, they are out there.'"

Phil Dunning, an attorney who has been frequenting the bar for two decades, called Trad'r Sam "seedy enough, but not too seedy." Dunning used to own a Mexican place around the corner. "The crowd is always entertaining," he said. "I'm the most boring guy in the place, which is my preference."

THE HEARTH, EST. 1967

4701 Geary Boulevard

Before he bought the Hearth at Eleventh Avenue and Geary, back when Sid Takemoto owned it, Ray Rex used to pull the 6:00 a.m. shift. He liked getting to work when most of the houses and flats in the neighborhood were still dark. The Hearth's drop ceiling, threadbare burgundy carpeting, back parlor, faux fireplace, and hushed conversation made it feel like a sanctuary in the neighborhood's fog.

"We'd go 'tap, tap, tap' on the window and he would open the door up," recalled Sam, a retired cop who still frequents the bar. The Hearth was a stop on the way home for a few Richmond Station night officers who commuted to Novato. It was their happy hour.

Today, Rex says, it's socially unacceptable to drink before noon. "Sid Takemoto was one of the last guys in the neighborhood who opened at 6:00 a.m.," he said. "We would have a full bar. Cops from Richmond Station. Workers from the twenty-four-hour Safeway. The original Boudin Bakery across the street. Everybody would be reading the newspaper. Watching CNN. Checking their stocks. The wives would call and say, 'Get me some milk.'"

Ray Rex is a Richmond guy through and through. He grew up at Forty-Fifth and Anza, the son of a machinist and homemaker who had emigrated from Germany. After high school he worked as a car mechanic, casino security staffer, nightclub

Owner Ray Rex

manager, and projectionist at the Coronet movie house on Geary. In 2003 he had been driving a cab in San Francisco for a few years when he took a second job bartending for Takemoto at the Hearth. By 2007, Takemoto, who had owned the place since 1966, decided to retire and sold it to Rex.

Rex is unapologetically "sentimental and nostalgic." He loves talking to the old-timers about their memories of the city. He can list a string of no-frills joints that have disappeared along Geary and Clement—Dizzy's, Fizzies, Tippy's, Pat O'Shea's, the Red Lion, Holy City Zoo, the Last Day Saloon. A few are still around, like Ireland's 32, the 540, and Would You Believe? but they cater to a young crowd.

One of the favorite topics of conversation at the Hearth is an incident that occurred on November 27, 1966, right before Takemoto bought the bar. That night three men walked in wearing blue suits and crisp white shirts. Their hair was fashionably long. Over the course of five hours they drank and played liar's dice. They were loud and obnoxious enough that John Kammeyer, the bar manager who was engaged to the previous owner, referred to them under his breath as "punks."

That might have been a mistake. At midnight the men pulled out guns: two pistols and a single-barrel 12-guage shotgun.

"What is this?" asked Kammeyer.

"This is *it*," responded William Williams, the leader of the trio.

Williams shot Kammeyer in the back and the gunmen dragged him bleeding across the bar to the closet-sized office, where they ordered him to open the safe. He was nearly unconscious and couldn't manage to tell them the combination. The bar's owner pleaded with one of the men, William Asher, to let her call an ambulance for her fiancé. They did not. Asher blamed his associate, Williams. "That punk is trigger happy. He is going to be sorry he did this," said Asher. Kammeyer did not survive.

All three men were charged with murder and were sentenced to life in prison. But in 1975 Asher escaped from a remote fire camp in El Dorado County. He made it to Canada, where he changed his identity, worked as a truck driver, and raised a family. Eventually, he divorced and settled with a new girlfriend in Salida, seventy miles south of Sacramento. That's where the FBI found him in 2011.

When news of the arrest broke, Hearth regulars celebrated with a round of shots and a frenzy of Internet sleuthing. "The arrest kind of opened a can of worms," said Rex. "Everybody started giving me stuff." Suddenly, he was inundated with literature related to the case—trial transcripts, newspaper clips, and historic photos. Who knew the place counted so many barstool historians among its regulars?

The interest the case generated among his customer base reaffirmed the commitment Rex has always felt to Takemoto and the bar's history. At the same time, Rex has not let the bar become stagnant. In recent years he has imbued the Hearth with a German flair and a menu of Bavarian beers, a tribute to his heritage. Bartender Meredith Godfrey hosts a monthly comedy night, "Meredith's Realty Check Extravaganza," with regular John Heaphy on sound. Rex met his fiancée, Janette, at the bar. He was hanging Christmas decorations. She walked in and, amused by what she saw as decorating deficiencies, basically told him where to put stuff. "We hit it off," Rex said.

Rex loves to throw a party. "People pick themselves up. They get their degrees. They fall in love," he said. "You don't want to see people drowning their sorrows. You want to see people celebrating. That is my joy. You might not see them for a while, but when you do it's in a celebratory mood. We are not going to solve your problems by drinking. We are going to celebrate life."

One night, Rex was pouring drinks behind the bar when a cab double-parked in front. A gentleman jumped out wearing a hospital gown, paper booties, an ID bracelet, and an IV hookup. It was Stanley, a regular. Stanley turned around to reveal that his butt cheeks were flapping in plain view behind the robe. The cabbie was honking his horn outside. Stanley had not paid his fare. "I said, 'Stanley, you know I can't serve you,'" recalled Rex. "He said, 'Goddamn it I came all this way and I need a drink.'"

When he got out of the hospital, Stanley, clouded by hospital-grade painkillers, didn't remember the excursion. But Rex takes pride in it. "To me that is the essence of a neighborhood bar. You're stuck in the hospital, going a little crazy. You want to get out. Where do you think of going? You want to go to your local. It's a primitive impulse."

LIVERPOOL LIL'S,
EST. 1973
2942 Lyon Street

It's not true that the ashtrays at Liverpool Lil's were bugged during the Cold War. Ralph Maher, who owned the place, swears it isn't.

It *is* true that the British-style pub across from the gate to the Presidio was a regular hangout for the officers from the Soviet consulate a few blocks away at Green and Baker—which at the time Assistant United States Attorney Robert C. Bonner called "KGB Headquarters West" and a "nest of spies." And it's also a fact that Lil's was a hangout for cops, namely the FBI, Secret Service, CIA, DEA, and SFPD. But if you believe Maher—and not everybody does—those guys just hung out at Lil's because they were friends of his, not because they were gathering intelligence over ale, bangers, and mash.

"A couple of those Russian colonels liked to drink," said Maher. "They liked to frequent a couple of joints in the neighborhood, including my joint. It was downtime. Nobody was working. No deals were made. It was too busy, too noisy. I look back and laugh because nothing ever happened down here and the Russians seemed like nice people. Although of course there was a little tension before it finally broke."

Maher was a decorated Vietnam combat vet from the Bronx when he showed up in San Francisco in 1969 working as a military exchange sales rep. The money wasn't that good, so along the way he picked up second and third jobs—he drove a cab and worked the door at some of the new "fern bars" like Perry's that were just popping up along then-sleepy Union Street.

He wanted to buy a bar in North Beach or downtown, but all he could afford was a dingy beer-and-wine place called the Lyon's Den by the eastern gate to the Presidio. It was bikers and "major care guys" sneaking out of the Letterman hospital across the street, which had one of the VA's best orthopedic and burn centers. "It was a shame. You could see that in the guys who came in here at night, missing limbs and really fucked up," he said. "It was rough and tumble. It was wild local guys, a drug crowd. I had Hells Angels riding in here on their choppers."

With the row of eucalyptus trees rustling across the street, the place felt bucolic for San Francisco. The floor was red brick. The walls were twelve-inch-wide barn planks. Maher added ochre and sepia stained glass in the front—"the chapel effect"—a mahogany bar, and red leather–upholstered bar stools. He kept the place dim and den-like, with red lighting. Without having spent much time in British pubs, Maher thought it felt like a place one might stumble upon in the English countryside.

"I didn't know what English pub food was. I had to ask my English friends. Boxty potatoes—what the hell's that? There are 1001 ways the English have to reconstitute the potato."

At first he wanted to call the place "Liverpool Lou's," the name of a ballad about a prostitute written by Dominic Behan,

Owner Eddie Savino

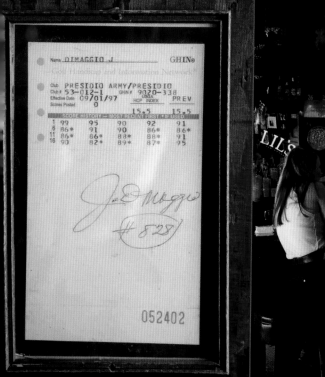

the brother of Brendan Behan. But Maher didn't know if that song was about an actual person (it turned out it wasn't), so he changed the name to Lil. "I used to say Liverpool Lil was Liverpool Lou's sister who worked the other side of the street."

Maher thought he would hold onto the place for two years and then sell it and buy a bar in North Beach. "I could count on my hands the number of people who were in here at any given time," he said. "My friends thought I was nuts. People would say, 'Let's go down and see if Ralph is still alive.' At least they knew there was plenty of parking."

An undercover narcotics cop friend of his chased out the drug dealers who were operating out of the apartment upstairs. Maher encouraged the resident Hells Angels leader to at least

find somewhere else to park their bikes. "I told him, 'You're killing me. People come by, see the bikes lined up, and they don't come in.' He looked at me and said, 'Don't worry, you wont see us again.' I figured he would put me in the ground. But he put the word out and none of his guys showed up again."

Lil's got a full liquor license on St. Patrick's Day, 1974, and the place got busier and busier. Maher opened the Brazen Head down on Buchanan Street and the Penny Farthing on Sutter Street.

The Marina took off. Joe DiMaggio was a regular at Liverpool Lil's. He would come in the afternoons—fitted jacket, starched shirt, spit-shined shoes—for a Pabst Blue Ribbon. The walls filled up with photos and memorabilia. Maher dismisses the décor as "general junk that came out of basements and garages." There is one piece of artwork he is fond of: a three-by-four drawing of Duke Ellington that Al Rudis did as a backdrop for the Monterey Jazz Festival, an event that regular Jimmy Lyons started and some of the Liverpool Lil's crowd volunteered at. "That has sentimental value," said Maher. "Duke was the supreme leader in jazz. Al was a wonderful cantankerous guy. And Jimmy kept jazz alive in the Bay Area."

In 2005 Maher sold Liverpool Lil's and the Brazen Head to Eddie Savino, who had worked at or managed both places. "It's a tough business, and very few places make it. Circumstances work against you. Leases, landlords, the economics. There are so many variables," he said. "It's rare that you start something and move on and forty years later can still come and back and feel comfortable."

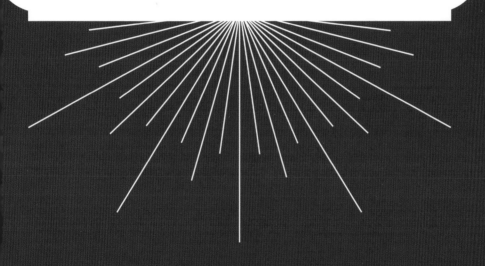

THE MARINA

MAUNA LOA, EST. 1939

3009 Fillmore Street

The Mauna Loa is rooted in a love affair that began in 1935, thousands of miles away amid volcanic volatility in Hawai'i. That year, as lava flows from the Mauna Loa volcano threatened the Hilo region, Johnny Martin fell in love with Marie Estes. Martin's Catholic parents frowned on the budding relationship because Marie was divorced and had two daughters from a previous marriage. As George S. Patton was leading a bombing operation to try to divert the lava flows from threatened villages, Martin and Estes were devising a plan of escape.

It worked. In early 1936 the lava flows stopped and the couple shipped out to San Francisco, got married, and sent for the girls. Upon arriving in San Francisco, Johnny got a job as a cook at Koko Brothers, Marie as a maid. They were married July 28, 1937. Diana and Bridget, ages four and six, arrived in August on the *SS Lurline* wearing their first sandals—island children wore no shoes.

In 1939, with the family reunited in San Francisco, Marie gave birth to another child, John Rene, and saved enough money to buy a bar at 3165 Steiner Street. Of course they named it the Mauna Loa.

The Marina District that Johnny and Marie settled into was different from today's. Down the hill from Pacific Heights' gold coast, the neighborhood had a strong middle-class community of first- and second-generation Italians for whom the Marina was a step up from North Beach's flats. Much of the housing in the flats was new, built on land filled in for use during the 1915 Panama-Pacific Exposition.

The bar was full of merchant marines, service men from the Presidio, Norwegian sailors staying up the street at the Norway House. What is now the back room of the bar was then a "swamper unit," where the maintenance man, or "swamper," found accommodations in exchange for work. The back door was connected by alley to a residential hotel, and the transient men who lived in the hotel accessed the Mauna Loa through the back door.

The Martins lived above the bar on the top floor. Marie attended mass at St. Vincent de Paul every day, and placed bets on the ponies with a bookie at Jurgerson's Market. At closing time, she would venture downstairs in bathrobe and slippers to collect the "bank," which she kept in a dresser drawer next to the rosary beads.

Since then, the bar, which moved around the corner in 1950 to 3009 Fillmore Street, has remained in the Martin family. The three kids attended school at St. Vincent de Paul, followed by St. Ignatius and University of San Francisco. "The whole Catholic run," said grandson Curt Martin.

After Johnny and Marie retired, ownership of the bar was taken over by Rene Martin, a teacher at Washington High School, and his sister Diana, who lived around the corner on Laguna. "Diana was a big character," said Martin. "She was that

Owner Curt Martin

kind of an old bar broad. She always wore a leather coat. She smoked. She drank. She had a filthy mouth."

Rene Martin raised his family in Daly City, but his son Curt Martin would often stay upstairs in his grandparents' spare room overlooking Fillmore Street. He remembers laughter from the barroom drifting up at night and the splashes of neon reflected on the bedroom walls. He remembers lunch at the Doggie Diner on the corner, the aisle of candy at Ici's Pharmacy. At the Mauna Loa "it was the underage and overserved," said Martin. "The windows were boarded up. Smoke was billowing out of the place. The plate-glass windows kept breaking, so they boarded them up."

Curt Martin turned twenty-one in 1983, and by 1985 or '86 he was gradually taking over the bar from his father and aunt. The Marina was changing fast. Union Street was becoming a dining and nightlife destination, with increasingly upscale bars and restaurants. The 1989 earthquake did not damage the Mauna Loa, but it accelerated changes already underway in the neighborhood. Seismic retrofitting allowed landlords to empty buildings of longtime rent-control tenants. In the Marina, 1,640 housing units were irreparably destroyed of damaged, 66 percent of which were rent controlled or residential hotels. Once the buildings were finally repaired a few years after the quake, many of the old-timers were long gone, replaced by a younger and more affluent demographic.

Martin knew the bar had to change with the times. He opened up the windows, turned the old swamper's quarters into game room—the Mauna Loa was the first bar in the city with the basketball game Pop-A-Shot—and started attracting a broader crowd of newcomers and restaurant workers, in addition to the born-and-raised neighborhood gang. A parquet bar counter was added in the 1980s, along with Toulouse Lautrec-esque wood carvings by Jean-Claude Gaugy, who drank in the bar and traded art for drinks.

Chef Tom Speirley

Martin recently moved upstairs above the bar after raising his kids in the East Bay. On football Sundays in the fall, and during bid sporting events like the World Cup and the World Series, Martin opens up the back patio and "Chef Tom"—Tom Spellicy, a chef at the Fairmont Hotel who moved to the neighborhood in the late 1980s—might go through sixty pounds of pulled pork, forty pounds of chicken, and thirty pounds of beef.

When Chef Tom turned fifty a friend offered to take him to a matinee and for drinks afterwards. Spellicy's one request? "Don't take me to the Mauna Loa." After all, he had been going there every weekend for twenty-five years. But his friend insisted they had to swing by to pick up a couple of friends. When they arrived, the windows were covered up with butcher paper. "I said, 'Geez, I hope it's not one of those pub crawls with funny customs and screaming kids,'" Spellicy said.

Inside, Martin had been busy. He had one of the beer distributors make up a banner that said "Happy Birthday Tommy." He had filled the room with Spellicy's friends—forty or fifty people, mostly regulars at the Mauna Loa. He had put out a spread of food on the back bar and hired a rock trio to play in the corner.

Chef Tom was genuinely shocked. "Curt has got one of the biggest hearts of anybody I have ever met," Spellicy said. "He is that kind of a guy, and this is that kind of a bar."

EPILOGUE

The bar owners profiled in this book are urban alchemists. They thrive at throwing parties, at generating buzz, at concocting social environments as unpredictable and magical as San Francisco itself.

Yet for all the imagination and creative spirit that goes into building a great bar, often the thing that proves fatal is something very different—the business of real estate.

Over the year I spent researching this book, I heard bar owners express, over and over, trepidation over whether their businesses would survive the seemingly unstoppable march of real estate speculation sweeping San Francisco, an environment in which every single-story retail building is a potential condo play and every neighborhood dive bar is a blueprint for a craft cocktail lounge makeover.

Two deeply rooted gay bars in the Mission closed while this book was being researched, Esta Noche and the Lexington Club, which the upscale PlumpJack Group agreed to buy in February of 2015. Other places like the Elbo Room (Valencia Street) and the Ave (Ocean Avenue) were slated to be knocked down to clear the way for housing. Still other buildings that house historic bars, including the homes of the EndUp and Mr. Bing's Cocktail Lounge, went on the market.

One historic restaurant and bar that went out of business as this book was being researched was the Empress of China, a Chinatown rooftop banquet hall and sky bar of faded 1960s *Flower Drum Song*-era chinoiserie, syrupy cocktails, and killer views clear across to Coit Tower and beyond. The Empress served its last mai tais on New Year's Eve 2014 as commercial real estate brokers were busy marketing the building for sale as creative office space for tech companies.

As much as hyper development and rising costs are to blame for the displacement of some legacy establishments, that is just part of it. Tastes change. Neighborhoods evolve. Bars and restaurants get left behind. This was a factor with the Empress of China. Opened by Kee Joon Lee in 1966 on the top two floors of a six-story building, the Empress was the center of a hopping Chinatown nightlife. The restaurant, bar, and nightclub boasted "an opulent atmosphere of dynastic splendor and elegance." Its garden court featured a pine tree, an overhead dome, and a fifty-ton wooden octagonal pavilion "inspired by the original creation in the royal pleasure park in Peking." The walls of the lobby were lined with faded pictures of Lee posing with celebrities. Senator Dianne Feinstein is there. So is Chuck Norris, Dick Cavett, Arnold Schwarzenegger, Lana Turner and Eric Estrada.

But as the heart of the city's Chinese population moved out to the Avenues and the suburbs, the neighborhood's nightlife waned. "Chinatown used to be alive," said Erika Marr-Pollasky, Lee's granddaughter and part of the ownership group. "The streets were full of people until after midnight. People from all over the city came to Chinatown to eat and dance. It has lost that over the years. We don't have a lot of regulars anymore. They have died and their children don't live here anymore."

It's possible, but not likely, that a restaurant operator will come along and revive the Empress of China's historic bones, making it feel fresh and relevant to contemporary Chinatown. That has happened in recent years with some of the city's classic places, including Café Du Nord and the Swedish American Music Hall in Upper Market, Tosca Café in North Beach, the Big Four on Nob Hill, the Dogpatch Saloon on Third Street, and two financial district spots, Schroeder's Restaurant on Front Street and the House of Shields on New Montgomery.

At the House of Shields, the 1908 tavern across from the Palace Hotel, Dennis Leary's group reupholstered booths and replaced hand-blown glass sconces. They fixed the busted mosaic-tiled floor and refinished all the woodwork—the hand-carved redwood bar, the wood-paneled walls, the classical statues of crones, maidens, and amazons.

To be sure, the meticulous restoration changed the customer base. Gone are the $2 Pabst Blue Ribbon cans and the bike messengers in cutoff shorts who had frequented the bar since the 1980s. The graffiti and rock band decals that adorned the woodwork have been removed. The bar's booths and mezzanine have become popular with downtown deal makers, executives from companies like Airbnb and Yelp, attorneys, guests at the Palace Hotel across the street. The bartenders wear white shirts and neckties and charge downtown prices.

Some lamented the changes as yet another sign that San Francisco is losing its soul to greed, but in reality the restoration brought the House of Shields back to what it was in the 1950s and 1960s when it was elbow-to-elbow *San Francisco*

Examiner staffers from the nearby Hearst Building and short-line railroad executives playing hooky from the Monadnock Building around the corner. "It was really run- down—corroded and dilapidated," said Leary. "It was a dive bar, but this really isn't a dive bar neighborhood."

That's a good point. San Francisco is home to 36 neighborhoods and 665 bars. The neighborhoods are constantly evolving. In some cases bars have to adapt or they will become superfluous. In other situations they have to resist change or their clientele will be resentful. Overall, San Francisco is lucky that it is full of people, natives and newcomers alike, who understand that there is value to be found in preserving continuity of culture and community at a time of rapid change. San Francisco Heritage's Legacy Bars and Restaurants project is a testament to that fact. So is this book. Places like Sam Jordan's, Trad'r Sam, Gino and Carlo, the Bus Stop, and the Mauna Loa have been passed down from generation to generation along with stories and traditions that grow ever richer with time. Other joints like Specs', Vesuvio Café, the Hotel Utah, the Wild Side West, the Philosopher's Club, and Aub Zam Zam remain true to their roots because a dedicated group of guardians—patrons, owners, and bartenders—would not have it any other way.

In a dense urban environment, where most of us live and work in cramped quarters, an attachment to a local tavern can become extremely personal. Bars often double as our public living rooms and community centers, places we go to celebrate anniversaries or graduations. One of the best lines I heard when researching this book came from Gregory Eliston, a retired postal worker who frequents Sam Jordan's in the Bayview District. Eliston was talking about how a lot of the neighborhood bars he frequented as a young man have vanished. You can't even find them on Google.

For that reason he was always reluctant to go to Sam's. Despite the fact that he knew all about its position as an important African American institution, he avoided it because he was afraid he would be disappointed. "Sooner or later a bar is gonna let you down—it ain't like having a piece of family," said Eliston. "You can almost smell a bar when it's dying."

But one day in 2004 he was walking by Sam Jordan's on Mother's Day. Clyde Colen, who is married to co-owner Ruth Jordan, was out on the sidewalk handing out red roses to women as they walked by. Eliston could hear the Stevie Wonder and smell the ribs from the smoker on the little concrete patio in back. "I thought, 'Yeah—I kinda like that,' and I walked in," he recalled.

A decade later, Eliston is thankful he did. He runs into people he worked with at the post office, people he went to school with, young people new to the city willing to share a smoke with him on the patio. He sees Sam Jordan's, like the twenty-five other bars profiled in this book, as a place that newcomers can come to for a taste of old San Francisco and city natives can return to for something familiar. Maybe it ain't like having "a piece of family." But it's not bad, he allowed. "Where else am I going to get a piece of fried catfish at 12:30 in the morning?" he said. "You can't take a place like Sam's for granted."

APPENDIX:

San Francisco Heritage's Certified Legacy Establishments

Alfred's Steak House, 1928
659 Merchant Street
San Francisco, CA 94111
415-781-7058
alfredssteakhouse.com

Alioto's Restaurant, 1925
8 Fisherman's Wharf
San Francisco, CA 94133
415-673-0183
aliotos.com

Anchor Steam Brewery, 1871
1705 Mariposa Street
San Francisco, CA 94107
415-863-8350
anchorbrewing.com

Aub Zam Zam, 1942
1633 Haight Street
San Francisco, CA 94117
415-861-2545

Balboa Café, 1913
3199 Fillmore Street
San Francisco, CA 94123
415-921-3944
balboacafe.com

Beep's Burgers, 1960s
1051 Ocean Avenue
San Francisco, CA 94112
415-584-2650

Benkyodo Company, 1906
1747 Buchanan Street
San Francisco, CA 94115
benkyodocompany.com

Bimbo's 365 Club, 1931
1025 Columbus Avenue
San Francisco, CA 94133
415-474-0465
bimbos365club.com

Buena Vista Café, 1916
2765 Hyde Street
San Francisco, CA 94109
415-474-5044

Bus Stop Bar, 1900
1901 Union Street
San Francisco, CA 94123
415-567-6905

Café Du Nord, 1907
2170 Market Street
San Francisco, CA 94114
415-861-5016
cafedunord.com

Café Flore, 1973
2298 Market Street
San Francisco, CA 94114
415-621-8579
cafeflore.com

Caffe Trieste, 1956
601 Vallejo Street
San Francisco, CA 94133
415-392-6739
caffetrieste.com

Casa Sanchez / Ayutla
Restaurant, 1924
2778 Twenty-Fourth Street
San Francisco, CA 94110
415-282-2400
casasanchezfood.com

Cha Cha Cha at Original
McCarthy's, 1933
2327 Mission Street
San Francisco, CA 94110
415-824-1502

Cliff House, 1863
1090 Point Lobos Avenue
San Francisco, CA 94121
415-386-3330
cliffhouse.com

Comstock Saloon, 1907
155 Columbus Avenue
San Francisco, CA 94133
415-617-0071
comstocksaloon.com

Dianda's Italian American Pastry, 1962
2883 Mission Street
San Francisco, CA 94110
415-647-5469
diandabakery.com

The Doctor's Lounge, 1951
4826 Mission Street
San Francisco, CA 94112
415-586-9730
doctorsloungesf.com

Dogpatch Saloon, 1912
2496 Third Street
San Francisco, CA 94107
415-643-8592
dogpatchsaloon.com

Double Play Bar and Grill, 1909
2401 Sixteenth Street
San Francisco, CA 94103
415-621-9859
doubleplaysf.com

Elbo Room, 1935
647 Valencia Street
San Francisco, CA 94110
415-552-1633
elbo.com

Elixir, 1858
3200 Sixteenth Street
San Francisco, CA 94103
415-552-1633
elixirsf.com

Empress of China, 1965
(CLOSED)
838 Grant Avenue
San Francisco, CA 94108

The EndUp, 1973
401 Sixth Street
San Francisco, CA 94103
415-646-0999
thendup.com/club

Far East Café, 1920
631 Grand Avenue
San Francisco, CA 94108
415-982-3245
fareastcafesf.com

Fior d'Italia, 1886
2237 Mason Street
San Francisco, CA 94133
415-986-1886
fior.com

Fishermen's Grotto, 1935
2847 Taylor Street
San Francisco, CA 94133
415-673-7025
fishermensgrotto.com

The Fly Trap, 1883
606 Folsom Street
San Francisco, CA 94107
415-243-0580
flytrapsf.com

Gangway, 1910
841 Larkin Street
San Francisco, CA 94109
415-776-6828

Garden Court, 1909
2 New Montgomery Street
San Francisco, CA 94105
415-546-5086
sfpalace.com/garden-court

Gino and Carlo, 1942
548 Green Street
San Francisco, CA 94133
415-421-0896
ginoamdcarlo.com

Gold Dust Lounge, 1967
165 Jefferson Street
San Francisco, CA 94133
415-397-1695
golddustsf.com

Gold Mirror Restaurant, 1969
800 Taraval Street
San Francisco, CA 94116
415-564-0401
goldmirrorrestaurant.com

Great American Music Hall, 1907
859 O'Farrell Street
San Francisco, CA 94109
415-885-0750
slimpresents.com/venue_detail/gamh

Grubstake, 1927
1525 Pine Street
San Francisco, CA 94109
415-673-8268
sfgrubstake.com

Hang Ah Tea Room, 1920
1 Pagoda Place
San Francisco, CA 94108

Ha-Ra Club, 1947
875 Geary Street
San Francisco, CA 94109
415-673-3148

Harrington's Bar and Grill, 1935
245 Front Street
San Francisco, CA 94111
415-392-7595
harringtonsbarandgrill.com

The Hearth, 1967
4701 Geary Boulevard
San Francisco, CA 94118
415-751-0200

Henry's Hunan Restaurant, 1974
924 Sansome Street
San Francisco, CA 94111
415-956-7727
henryshunanrestaurant.com

Hi Dive, 1916
Pier 28, The Embarcadero
San Francisco, CA 94105
415-977-0170
hidivesf.com

The Homestead, 1902
2301 Folsom Street
San Francisco, CA 94110
415-282-4663
homesteadsf.com

Horseshoe Tavern, 1934
2024 Chestnut Street
415-346-1430

The Hotel Utah, 1908
500 Fourth Street
San Francisco, CA 94107
415-546-6300
hotelutah.com

House of Prime Rib, 1949
1906 Van Ness Avenue
San Francisco, CA 94109
415-885-4605
houseofprimerib.net

House of Shields, 1908
39 New Montgomery Street
San Francisco, CA 94105
415-284-9958
thehouseofshields.com

It's Tops Coffee Shop, 1935
1801 Market Street
San Francisco, CA 94103
415-431-6395
itstopcoffeeshop.com

Java House, 1912
Pier 40, The Embarcadero
San Francisco, CA 94107
415-495-7260
javahousesf.com

John's Grill, 1908
63 Ellis Street
San Francisco, CA 94102
415-986-3274
johnsgrill.com

La Rocca's Corner, 1930s
957 Columbus Avenue
San Francisco, CA 94133
415-674-1266

Le Central, 1974
453 Bush Street
San Francisco, CA 94108
415-391-2233
lecentralbustro.com

Lefty O'Doul's, 1958
333 Geary Street
San Francisco, CA 94102
415-982-8900
leftyodouls.biz

Liguria Bakery, 1911
1700 Stockton Street
San Francisco, CA 94133
415-421-3786

Little Shamrock, 1890s
807 Lincoln Way
San Francisco, CA 94122
415-661-0060

Liverpool Lil's, 1973
2942 Lyon Street
San Francisco, CA 94123
415-921-6664
liverpolllils.com

Manor Coffee Shop, 1967
321 West Portal Avenue #A
San Francisco, CA 94127
415-661-2468

Mario's Bohemian Cigar Store
Café, 1971
566 Columbus Ave
San Francisco, CA 94133
415-362-0536

Mauna Loa, 1939
3009 Fillmore Street
San Francisco, CA 94123
415-563-5137

May's Coffee Shop, 1973
1737 Post Street
San Francisco, CA 94115
415-346-4020

Mitchell's Ice Cream, 1953
688 San Jose Avenue
San Francisco, CA 94110
415-648-2300

Mr. Bing's Cocktail Lounge, 1967
201 Columbus Avenue
San Francisco, CA 94133
415-362-1545

Northstar Café, 1882
1560 Powell Street
San Francisco, CA 94133
415-397-0577

Old Clam House, 1861
299 Bayshore Boulevard
San Francisco, CA 94124
415-826-4880
theoldclamhousesf.com

Old Ship Saloon, 1851
298 Pacific Avenue
San Francisco, CA 94111
415-788-2222
oldshipsaloon.com

Original Joe's, 1937
601 Union Street
San Francisco, CA 94133
415-775-4877
originaljoessf.com

Perry's, 1969
1944 Union Street
San Francisco, CA 94123
415-922-9022
perryssf.com

Philosophers Club, 1960
824 Ulloa Street
San Francisco, CA 94127
415-753-0599

The Pied Piper Bar and Grill,
1909
2 New Montgomery Street
San Francisco, CA 94105
415-546-5089
sfpalace.com/pied-piper

Pier 23 Café, 1937
Pier 23, The Embarcadero
San Francisco, CA 94111
415-362-5125
pier23cafe.com

Pop's Bar, 1935
2800 Twenty-Fourth Street
San Francisco, CA 94110
415-872-5160
popssf.com

The Ramp, 1950
855 Terry A. Francois Boulevard
San Francisco, CA 94107
415-621-2378
theramprestaurant.com

Red's Java House, 1930s
Pier 30, The Embarcadero
San Francisco, CA 94105
415-777-5626
redsjavahouse.com

Red's Place, 1940s
672 Jackson Street
San Francisco, CA 94108
415-956-4490
redsplacesf.com

Roosevelt Tamale Parlor, 1919
2817 Twenty-Fourth Street
San Francisco, CA 94110
415-824-2600

Sabella and La Torre, 1927
2809 Taylor Street
San Francisco, CA 94133
415-673-2824
sabellalatorre.com

The Saloon, 1861
1232 Grant Avenue
San Francisco, CA 94133
415-989-7666

Sam's Grill, 1867
374 Bush Street
San Francisco, CA 94104
415-421-0594
belden-place/samsgrill

Sam Jordan's Bar and Grill, 1959
4004 Third Street
San Francisco, CA 94123
415-282-4003

Sam Wo, 1912 (CLOSED)
813 Washington Street
San Francisco, CA 94108

Sausage Factory, 1968
517 Castro Street
San Francisco, CA 94114
415-626-1250
castrosausagefactory.com

Schroeder's Restaurant, 1893
240 Front Street
San Francisco, CA 94111
415-421-4778
schroederssf.com

Sears Fine Food, 1938
439 Powell Street
San Francisco, CA 94102
415-986-0700
searsfinefood.com

Silver Crest Donut Shop, 1970
340 Bayshore Boulevard
San Francisco, CA 94124
415-826-0753

Specs' Twelve Adler Museum
Café, 1968
12 Saroyan Place
San Francisco, CA 94133
415-421-4112

St. Francis Fountain, 1918
2801 Twenty-Fourth Street
San Francisco, CA 94110
415-826-4210
stfrancisfountainsf.com

Swan Oyster Depot, 1912
1517 Polk Street
San Francisco, CA 94109
415-673-1101

Tadich Grill, 1849
240 California Street
San Francisco, CA 94111
415-391-1849
tadichgrill.com

Taquería La Cumbre, 1972
515 Valencia Street
San Francisco, CA 94110
415-863-8205
taquerialacumbre.com

Terry's Lodge, 1973
1368 Irving Street
San Francisco, CA 94122
415-731-1200

Thanh Long, 1971
4101 Judah Street
San Francisco, CA 94122
415-665-1146

Tommaso's Italian Restaurant,
1935
1042 Kearny Street
San Francisco, CA 94133
415-398-9696
tommasos.com

Tommy's Joynt, 1947
1101 Geary Boulevard
San Francisco, CA 94109
415-775-4216
tommysjoynt.com

Tommy's Mexican Restaurant,
1965
5929 Geary Boulevard
San Francisco, CA 94121
415-387-4747
tommysmexican.com

Tonga Room and Hurricane
Bar, 1945
950 Mason Street
San Francisco, CA 94108
415-772-5278
tongaroom.com

Tony Nik's, 1933
1534 Stockton Street
San Francisco, CA 94133
415-693-0990
tonyniks.com

Top of the Mark, 1939
999 California Street
San Francisco, CA 94108
415-616-6916
intercontinentalmarkhopkins
.com/top-of-the-mark.aspx

Tosca Café, 1920
242 Columbus Avenue
San Francisco, CA 94133
415-986-9651
toscacafesf.com

Trad'r Sam, 1937
6150 Geary Boulevard
San Francisco, CA 94121
415-221-0773

Twin Peaks Tavern, 1972
401 Castro Street
San Francisco, CA 94114
415-864-9470
twinpeakstavern.com

Vesuvio Café, 1948
255 Columbus Avenue
San Francisco, CA 94133
415-362-3370
vesuvio.com

The Wild Side West, 1962
424 Cortland Avenue
San Francisco, CA 94110
415-647-3099
wildsidewest.com

Whiz Burger, 1955
700 South Van Ness Avenue
San Francisco, CA 94110
415-824-5888

Since 1971, San Francisco Heritage, or "Heritage," has been leading the civic discussion about the compatibility of rapid change with protecting our past. Built on its activist underpinnings, Heritage has been instrumental in establishing the preservation protections that have allowed San Francisco to evolve and flourish. Heritage is a nonprofit 501(c)(3) membership organization with a mission to preserve and enhance San Francisco's unique architectural and cultural identity.

www.sfheritage.org

ABOUT THE AUTHOR

Photo by Spencer Brown

J. K. Dineen is a metro reporter at the *San Francisco Chronicle*, where he writes about real estate development, the waterfront, housing, neighborhoods, and land-use planning. He has also been a staff reporter at the *San Francisco Business Times, The San Francisco Examiner*, the *New York Daily News*, and a bunch of papers in his native Massachusetts. He is the author of *Here Tomorrow* (Heyday, 2013), a book about historic preservation in California. He lives in San Francisco with his family.

PHOTOGRAPH CREDITS

Photographs © 2015 by Spencer Brown: Vesuvio Café, Specs' Twelve Adler Museum Café (except for image at top of page 12), The Saloon, La Rocca's Corner, Mr. Bing's Cocktail Lounge, Lefty O'Doul's, The EndUp, The Hotel Utah, Cha Cha Cha at Original McCarthy's, Double Play Bar and Grill, Twin Peaks Tavern, Sam Jordan's Bar and Grill, The Ramp, The Wild Side West, Aub Zam Zam, Mauna Loa

Photographs ©2015 by Cindy Chew: Gangway, The Pied Piper Bar and Grill, Hi Dive, Elixir, The Homestead, Silver Crest Donut Shop, Trad'r Sam, The Hearth, Liverpool Lil's

Photographs © 2015 by Paolo Vescia: Philosophers Club, and image of Specs at top of page 12

HEYDAY
into California

ABOUT HEYDAY

Heyday is an independent, nonprofit publisher and unique cultural institution. We promote widespread awareness and celebration of California's many cultures, landscapes, and boundary-breaking ideas. Through our well-crafted books, public events, and innovative outreach programs we are building a vibrant community of readers, writers, and thinkers.

THANK YOU

It takes the collective effort of many to create a thriving literary culture. We are thankful to all the thoughtful people we have the privilege to engage with. Cheers to our writers, artists, editors, storytellers, designers, printers, bookstores, critics, cultural organizations, readers, and book lovers everywhere!

We are especially grateful for the generous funding we've received for our publications and programs during the past year from foundations and hundreds of individual donors. Major supporters include:

Alliance for California Traditional Arts; Anonymous (6); Arkay Foundation; Judith and Phillip Auth; Judy Avery; Carol Baird and Alan Harper; Paul Bancroft III; The Bancroft Library; Richard and Rickie Ann Baum; BayTree Fund; S. D. Bechtel, Jr. Foundation; Jean and Fred Berensmeier; Berkeley Civic Arts Program and Civic Arts Commission; Joan Berman; Nancy Bertelsen; Barbara Boucke; Beatrice Bowles, in memory of Susan S. Lake; John Briscoe; David Brower Center; Lewis and Sheana Butler; Helen Cagampang; California Historical Society; California Indian Heritage Center Foundation; California State Parks Foundation; Joanne Campbell; The Campbell Foundation; James and Margaret Chapin; Graham Chisholm; The Christensen Fund; Jon Christensen; Cynthia Clarke; Community Futures Collective; Lawrence Crooks; Lauren and Alan Dachs; Nik Dehejia; Topher Delaney; Chris Desser and Kirk Marckwald; Lokelani

GETTING INVOLVED

To learn more about our publications, events, membership club, and other ways you can participate, please visit www.heydaybooks.com.